A Graphic Textbook

Drawing the Practice of Social Work

By: Jed Metzger

LINUS
Learning

Published by Linus Learning
Ronkonkoma, NY 11779

ISBN 10: 1-60797-703-6

ISBN 13:978-1-60797-703-2

Printed in the United States of America.

Print Numbers   5   4   3   2   1

Introduction

Intention, and clarity of purpose, these are important concepts for us as social work practitioners. It is hard to imagine that anyone has gotten through social work graduate school without having to explain how come they were becoming a professional social worker. By the same token most social workers who do direct practice can recall several if not more stories of needing to respond to the people we might call our clients as to our intention with them, with their information or their family. As such there is a real need to be clear about the intention of this book. Let's face it; there are already enough textbooks of social work practice, why do we need one more? Simply repackaging the same information seems an insufficient rational for the use of the paper much less the money. In direct language the intention of this book is to be *useful* in a way that textbooks often cannot. You will find that while there is a lot of information in this book, it is not "dumped" on you so that you can memorize it, it will be related to you so you can think about it. This book uses stories and drawings to "teach". This approach is used because there is real evidence that in our postmodern world where so much (too much) information is directed at our often over worked brains, that stories and pictures are retained better (Brown, Roediger & McDaniel, 2014). You will note that the last sentence had a citation; efforts will be made to limit the in-text citation and include important readings at the end of chapters, but some sentences need support so as not to come across as some un-fact checked political claim.

Conceptually any book of social work practice, once read, should lead to the reader being better able to practice social work. In this way the book is *helpful*. This book is trying to be *useful*. Being useful is a related but different idea. This is not to say that textbooks are not helpful, by all means find a good one or two and read it. The explanation of the ins and outs of the various models and approaches are good fundamental knowledge. This book is intended to be a companion to those textbooks. This book is less interested in the "what" of social work practice and more interested in the "how" of social work practice. This book makes no claim against the importance of evidence-based practice or the critical nature of fidelity of the various models, all which is true. However this book aims at being directly useful. In multiple studies when researchers ask the people that social workers work with, what made it work? The top answer repeatedly is "how they were with me". That is what is meant by being useful. The intention of this book is to explore how we can more successfully do *that thing* and thereby be useful to the reader. In addition as the intention of this book is not so much to disseminate information as to provoke thought, the chapters are short, they need not necessarily be read in any particular order and they are intended to be the kind of writing that a person may want to return to. One of the things I have always loved about social work is I can always get better at it. Each new person I work with tends to teach me something. Like an Evergreen, it is always in bloom.

The idea being is to not read this book to get through it and be done with it, but to use it to provoke your social work practice to a deeper and more connected place.

From the late 1960's through the early 1980's the Baltimore Orioles baseball team was managed by a cantankerous man named Earl Weaver. His approach on the field and his relationships towards his players have never seemed like good role models for social workers, but his philosophy, best put in the title of one of his books "It is what I learned after I knew it all" really is consistent with the type of approach to our work that this book strives to explore. It is believed that excellence as a social work practitioner is not so much about what you know; it is about the way you are with people. So use your text books to learn everything you need to know and then use this book to take that further and find out how to be useful to the people you have the honor and privilege to work with. While it is common in this introductory space to review the chapters, the reader is directed to the index as most of the topics covered are self-explanatory, and the topics that are not self-explanatory hopefully invite enough curiosity that you will read them as well. A note on the drawings is perhaps in order. The drawings are crude, untrained, sometimes requiring an explanation to decipher but hopefully they provoke a sense of humor and mostly are memorable. What we know about the way our brain store information is that the image center develops sooner and has a longer shelf life. The drawings are meant to provoke you to think about your approach in the area being considered, they are the piece of string tied around your finger pictured below to remember to get that quart of milk at the grocery store. If you can draw a better one, do so, it will be more useful most certainly.

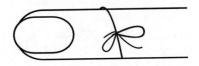

Brown, P., Roediger, H. & McDaniel, M. (2014). Make it Stick: The Science of Successful Learning. Belknap Press: Cambridge, MA.

Dedication

This book would not be possible without my teachers: In New York, my field instructor, Denise R., and the axis of good supervisors at JCCA- Sue G., Dr. B and Dr. F., in Rochester - Bill, Bill and Dr. Gene. And the most important teachers of all: the children, youth and families I have had the deep honor of serving. I am grateful for my loving parents, my sister and brother, my beautiful wife, and two amazing daughters. This project was written and drawn to the musical inspiration of the good old G.D.

Index of Chapters

Be where the person is at

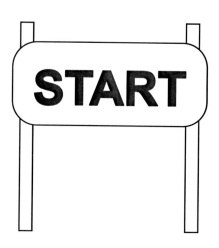

In graduate school in your first practice class, no doubt you were told that good practice demands that you start where the person is at. Starting where a person is at and staying in that place with them really is the best way to meet their real needs. This is of course easier said than done. What we are talking about here is engagement, actually continuous engagement. We get tripped up when we think about engagement as a thing that we complete. Engagement with others is a fragile thing, it is special and it should be treated as such. The more you can stay attentive to the relationship you are building, the better you will see where the person you are working with is at. Experience has shown that the minute we take for granted that we are engaged, is the minute that we invite in disaster because we are no longer totally focusing on where the person is at. The question is, how to do train yourself to have that intense focus? How to you train yourself to consistently actively listen? One way is to start by acknowledging to yourself that this type of intense focusing is hard, it is physically and mentally draining. Give yourself credit for engaging in such a rigorous profession. A second tip is to use a cognitive-behavioral technique of "thought-stopping" in which you imagine a Stop sign anytime your mind starts to wander. Being able to conjure up the shape, color and letters and directly letting that be your warning to get off the side track and get back onto the focus on being with the person who is right in front of you, is a concrete way to stay focused.

In truth often times it is hard to know what the point is, the conversation may seem to be meandering, you may find the person frustrating or not that appealing. You may not feel that you should have gotten this case. It is in these moments that I directly suggest you think about those horses at the starting gate and ask yourself to intently focus in what is going on for them. If you do not know, it is good to just say "hold on, I am lost, explain it to me again" The idea is that the more we can lean into the person(s) we are working with intensity and curious, respectful purpose, the greater the likelihood of positive engagement.

One idea to help keep us focused on engagement is to make sure that part of what we talk about is how it is going with us. Professionally we call this *making the content be the process*. By this I mean that I directly encourage you to ask the person you are working with, how this thing we are doing is going? Is this working for them? If so how? If not, how come? In either case, what would make it better? This may seem awkward at first but by making at least some of what you talk about, how working together is going builds trust and gives you a direct way to be sure you are where they are right now.

Think of it this way, imagine you are in a lineup, you know the kind they use on the police shows and the witness has to pick the suspect out, well imagine you are in a lineup like that, except all the folks are other social workers, would the person you are currently working with pick you out? Maybe, maybe not, but now they got you and you got them. I see this as a gift, really like some giant act of random kindness. I never know who will be assigned to me, but I do treat it like a magical gift that we got brought together. At the same time, it is essential to ask how it is going talking to me about the things that you are talking about. In this way you make some of the content be your process, and that helps with engagement.

Do not get ahead of the person AKA the Onion & the Knife

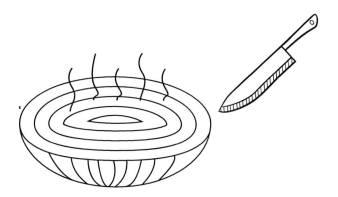

This is a picture of an onion cut in half by a knife. Onions are part of the Allium family. As such they have a chemical that when released close to the human eye can make tears come. You can try this out, take a fresh onion hold it close to your face and cut it in half, being careful not to injure yourself. Did you cry? Now take another equally fresh onion and hold it close to your face but this time carefully peel it one layer at a time. Start with the brownish outer paper like layers and work your way inward through the thin translucent layers and the thicker white layers. Did you cry? Usually you will not have cried with the slow peeling approach. That is a lot like social work. The people we work with often are not in graduate school, they may not see some of the challenges in their own life as clearly or quickly as you do. When we go too fast, when we get ahead of the people we are working with, we risk our connection and really are not that useful to them. The idea is not for *you* to know, it is for *them* to know through a process with you. You want them to lead. Use your ability to ask curious questions so they stay in front of the work. Peel the onion slowly, don't chop it – that just makes tears. While sometimes there has to be tears, but try to have them not come because we were rushing the process. It is about having the trust that given the time and a safe space with you, that people will come to the understanding that they need. Again, if you can see ahead, use that to help with your curiosity but it will be so much more meaningful to the person if they come to the answer themselves than if you tell them. This is another way we demonstrate respectful engagement by giving them to time to figure themselves out. It is amazing really when you are working with someone, and they say "you know what? I just thought of something" and then they go on to tell you about an understanding they have had. An understanding that they are willing to share with you, now you are sharing that understanding together, but it is there's to bring to you, not ours to tell them about. Let this be an mantra "Peel the onion slowly".

Engagement part one: Advanced empathy

In an effort to not gloss over engagement, or have it seem like it is something we do and then move on, we will break down the various core aspects that makes for good continuous engagement. The first is advanced empathy. The idea that empathy is central to engagement probably comes as no surprise. We understand empathy as the ability to sense what it is like to walk in someone else's shoes.

Advanced empathy is being able to sense what it is like to walk in someone else's shoes plus the ability to reflect that sense back to the person with enough intensity so they believe we get it, that we get what it is like to be them. Perhaps a story is the best way I can illustrate this. For ten years I was the clinical administrator for three group homes for youth with emotional, behavioral, family and mental health challenges. One home was for teenage boys who were placed by the family court. The homes were staffed around the clock and each had a professional social worker. Into this home we got a young man, who came in with his mother effectively gone from his life for several years, "lost to the streets and drugs" was what we were told and whose father was eight years into serving 25 to life on a murder charge. About six weeks after the young man moved in with us the social worker got a call from the father, he had been released that day due to a technicality in the way the evidence had been handled in his trial and he wanted his son. The social worker was immediately thrilled and told the father so and that he would set up visits and work towards reunification. The father cut him off with "no I am coming today and taking him". The next two minutes the conversation deteriorated quickly into expletives and threats, before the social worker told the father to get some air and call back later. The next day the father called again and again the conversation went south immediately but before getting off the phone, the father informed the social worker that he demanded a meeting with his supervisor the next day. The next day the father came in, although I introduced myself, the father started in on the social worker, after listening for a minute, I interrupted with "the social worker tells me you just got out of prison?" The father looked at me like a bull seeing red and tersely said "yes". I asked him how many prisons he had been in (knowing they tend to move people around). Counting on his fingers, he said "eight". I followed with "which one was hardest to do time in?" He named a prison, I countered with, "I expected you to say a different one". Father said his choice truly was the worst. I asked how come. Father told me about the sadism of the guards and the warden. I next asked him how did he survive his time that prison? "By thinking about my son", he said. By this time all the rage was gone from his voice. I commented that it told me a lot about his desire to be a dad as well as his toughness to survive in a brutal environment. He talked some more about how difficult it was in prison, not sure where his son was or what he was doing, if his son was safe, and how much he wanted to be a dad to his boy. The thing is I needed to get close to him. That is what engagement is. When working as a social worker and using any kind of relational approach, empathy is going to be the cornerstone of the continuous process that defines engagement. Let me be clear, he had killed a man. He was doing roofing work. Tearing old roofs off is hot, physical and dirty work; by its nature it is dangerous. Most folks, if they have a choice just would not do it. On a hot summer day, the man got into an argument with another fellow he was working with and killed him in the middle of the street with his roofing axe. I don't know anything about committing murder and I don't know anything about what it is like to have to do 25 to life in a brutal prison, I have never been to jail, not one day, but I needed to get close to understanding what it is like to have that be my reality with enough intensity that he believed I could relate. The practice skill here is to move beyond saying "I know what you mean", because that clearly just is not true and would sound fake. The way to get there is to using your curious questions to get into the heart of the matter, so you can understand it and then you need to be able to reflect back with enough intensity that the person believes you are interested in them. I only needed a few, nothing real brilliant: (1-how many prisons? 2- Which was hardest? 3) How come it was hardest? 4- How did you get through it?). You do not have to have all the answers or have experienced all the experiences, what you need to demonstrate is a willingness to get next to the other person's reality without judgement, by using simple deep curiosity. In sum, empathy is being able to know what it is like to be in someone else's shoes, advanced empathy is being able to reflect that sense back to them with enough intensity so they believe you. If you can practice social work with advanced empathy, your engagement will consistently deepen.

Engagement part two: The respectful stance

Similar to basic and advanced empathy, being respectful has long been a part of any good social work practice discussion. The challenge here is not so much in defining what respect is, but in maintaining an active practice of the many ways we demonstrate a respectful stance to the people we are working with. One way we do this is by promoting our core ethical stance of self-determination. Our Code directs us to the idea that people know what is best for them (NASW, 1999). We have to believe this in the face of them making what, by all appearances, looks like bad choices. One way to get to a respectful stance is to believe that all people are doing the best they can, that their choices reflect what makes most sense to them at the time. For instance my practice with youth has led to innumerable conversations about the relationship some youth have with marijuana. Kids don't need me to tell them not to smoke, not to get high, they don't need me to tell them that it is illegal (at least in my state) and they do not need to feel judged from me. At the same time, I do ask them "how is smoking weed working for you", "what do they like about getting high" and "what are the ways that weed gets you to do things you might not otherwise do?". Fact is that most every person that I have ever known that stopped smoking pot did so because they decided to do so. Not because their parents, a judge or a social worker told them to. They decided, for their own reasons that they no longer wanted weed in their life. Self-determination means we communicate to them that they have to be the captain of their own ship. That is what respect is; it is a communication that you can make the best decision for yourself. Not the decision I would make or that others want you to make, you can make the decision. I directly talk about dilemmas all the time. I might say "the court wants you to do X, but you don't want to do X, walk me through how you are going to handle this dilemma". The idea here is that most people know what is best for them, they do not always want to do it, but they know what the "right" answer is. They do not need me to remind them of what they already know; I am willing to bet that there are already plenty of people in their life offering the "right" advice. As a person trying to communicate a respectful stance, I offer an opportunity to weigh the choices without judgement.

A second way is that we demonstrate a respectful stance is to not skip the step of our confidentiality rap. Every place you work, with every population you work with, the boundaries of confidentiality may be a little different. The only respectful thing to do is to be straight with people is to tell them right from the beginning of our work together what the limits of confidentiality are in the setting where you practice. If you are not 100% confident on this, please put the book down, go into the bathroom, look into the mirror and practice your rap so it sounds authentic and not a canned speech. In reality you have to believe it in order to do it. By practicing it at home you will sound natural and believable. Remember, often times the people we work with are unsure about our intentions with them, being able to be direct about the limits of our relationship helps to set a respectful boundary for our time together. Respect is built on trust. I am direct with people, if I have a concern, I will tell them directly. I let people know that I am a mandated reporter. The truth is that my practice has always been with children, youth and families that face a lot of challenges. One thing that has been true is that sometimes the parenting decisions cross the line of what our society has determined to be neglectful or abusive. Often times that line is fairly murky, but it is our job to let people know if we feel we are legally mandated to report them, we will do just that. The only exception would be a personal safety issue, where the situation of me informing them that I must call has the potential to cause aggression be directed back at me, but I always want to let people know "I called, I had to, but I called". This is critical, because it allows space for respect. I can say "I don't think you are neglectful or abusive, I think you love your kids, I believe that you would prefer to be doing different things with them, but this is the law and I follow it and I am letting you know so you know I am straight with you". This is not an easy conversation and folks are often not happy with me in the moment, but over time, in more cases than not, we are able to get past it. They come to see my intention and feel the respect I have for them as people. This builds engagement.

A third way we demonstrate a respectful stance is by showing acceptance for their expressed emotion. Everyone gets mad, glad, and sad; many of us get jealous, spiteful, grumpy, intolerant and so forth. Our job is not to correct emotion, but to sit with it, allow emotion and seek to understand the emotion. Ask yourself, what is behind the emotion? Or what would make a person feel that way? When you ask yourself these types of questions it helps to position you so that you avoid judging or trying to change (fix) the emotion. Then all you need to do is acknowledge it, "it makes sense to me that you are pissed off". This will allow them to explore their emotion with you and not suppress their real emotion. It has got to be ok to be angry since everyone gets angry, communicate that there is nothing wrong with their emotion as long as they express it safely. In short if we tell people that they can talk about whatever they want, then we need to demonstrate that we can handle them talking about whatever they want. We do that by demonstrating acceptance for their expressed emotion.

A fourth way is to not argue in your own head about what is being presented to you. Assessment (as we will discuss) is a critical skill, but spending a lot of mental energy trying to decide if someone is lying to you will drain your engagement. One idea is to not think anyone is lying to YOU, instead that they are telling you a story. This then provides some space for you to think about how come they may believe they need to tell you or even themselves a story about the "truth". If I think someone is lying to me, then they are doing something to me I don't like, because I don't like being lied to. By reframing it away from a personal affront, I save room for our connection. There may be lots of reasons how come a person may be telling a story; they may believe it themselves, they may want to save face, they may think it is important to tell me what I want to hear, they may be concerned about the relative power I have over them, lots of really good reasons to tell a story. By not getting tripped up that I am being "done to", I stay open to trying to understand how come they are telling the story and it is so much better to be interested in that then by being on a constant hunt for the "truth". This work asks you to understand, not feel like you are on the latest episode of CSI. Again perhaps a story can illustrate this. For years we ran a camp for children who had lost a parent (s) to HIV/AIDS. Some of the counselors of the camp were the teenagers who had lost parents or who were HIV+ themselves. We would come to the camp a couple days early with the teens and other counselors (often some of my social work students) to train and set up the camp. I was driving a 16 year old girl up to camp and she disclosed to me that she was three months pregnant. We talked about it some. She let me know that while she had not planned on being a mom so young, or was really interested in the young man who was the bay's father, she was feeling like she could be a good mom. Her own dad was gone and her mom ravaged by the toll of being HIV+ for many years, she let me know that she had first-hand knowledge that life is short and you had to make the best of it. A couple nights later we were having a midnight campfire with all the teen counselor girls. We would often do this at the end of the day to decompress and give the teens a chance to rap about whatever was on their minds, good group work in essence. This night when one girl started a conversation that went something like "I know I act like I am a certain kind of way doing all these guys and such but actually I am a virgin". Then around the circle one girl after another admitted that they were a virgin too. The circle came to the girl I had driven up and she said she was a virgin too. My job at that moment was not to say "hey I thought you just told me you were pregnant" but rather to think about the circumstance and understand her need to belong to feel safe to be like the rest, and just practice acceptance. The message here is to try to not get caught up in a dogged search for the truth, especially if that search gets in the way of respectful engagement.

Engagement part three: Protecting our own warmth

Warmth is a fundamental building block to good engagement. The easy part of this aspect of engagement practice is that there is real value in being warm with the people you work with. As our society speeds up civility seems to be less and less apparent. In America watch how we drive and the amount of civility verses irritation, anger, and rage you see on the roads. Watch how often people are on their phones while in a checkout line at the grocery store, instead of chatting with the teller. A friend of mine is a railroad conductor; he tells me people no longer even look at him when he comes through for tickets. While we accept these societal changes they do leave little bruises, as service providers, when we bring warmth we set a different tone. This is a simple as just being happy to see the people you work with- even if that last session had been difficult. It is a handshake, a fist bump, an inquiry about a pet or a family member that demonstrates warmth. The good news here is that overwhelmingly social workers are warm people. You would not be in this line of work if you were not drawn in some way to human interaction. That said, this chapter will be more the issues that gets in the way of your being warm and how to keep those forces at bay so you can be you. So this chapter is not about suggestions on how to be warm, you already got that; it is about how to be ready to be warm.

One method is to have a mini preparation check in with yourself. This can take many forms. You may want to review your last exchange by reading your notes so you recall what you were talking about the last time you were together, or even just spending a moment to think about that person or family- trying to connect in your mind with them, with the way they move, talk, their expressions, and nuances. This may even take the form of you closing your door and taking a few deep breaths with your eyes closed. Do not ever underestimate the emotional load that our work demands of us, those brief moments to re-center ourselves help us stay warm and ready. While everyone is different, so many social workers I know report that what gets in the way of them being warm is the volume of the work. That their mind drifts to the phone calls to return, the list of e-mails to go through, the paperwork that they are behind on, the two people they need to check with before the end of the day and all of the sudden they are not in the room with the person in front of them or they are in "getting through this mode". The good news is that you are able to do something about staying warm. The more you have an active strategy the better you are positioned to stay present and warm. The idea here is to not take our warmth for granted. As simple as it sounds, the fact that you are warm does not matter if that warmth is not present. Below is a second drawing of a finger with a string tied to it. Below the drawing is a space, as goofy as it may be, in that space write yourself a note about what your strategy is to stay warm. When we write it down, we make it happen!

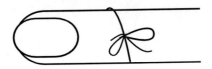

My plan to stay warm:

1)

2)

3)

4)

Engagement part four: Being real

This may be a controversial chapter for some, I will warn you in advance, but let me tell you the development of my thinking in this area. I did my MSW in New York City (the PhD in Clinical Social Work there too, but that was later on). After graduating with my MSW I was super lucky to get a job in an agency where I worked for the next nine years. One of the super aspects of the job was the supervision. I had a fantastic social worker as my main supervisor, a Swiss psychiatrist for clinical consultation and a psychologist who was a dead ringer for Al Pacino, to supervise my group work. The thing is that all three were classically trained psychoanalysts. So no pictures of family, friends, or vacations in the office, the psychologist took off his wedding room when he got to work each day. I was trained to not answer personal questions, but rather to always explore the meaning behind the questions. This is consistent with traditional Freudian approach (see *An Outline of Psychoanalysis, 1949*, Norton, for more detail), and really should be applied in any situation where a psychoanalytic approach is being provided. The question is, if we are not doing psychoanalysis, should we hold to this strict approach? I am making the suggestion that you keep good boundaries but be real. Specifically that the people you work with need to know that you are not a robot doing something you learned from a book, they need to believe that you are a person too. So if a person asks me if I am a parent, I say "yes I have two girls and I have found that parenting is the hardest job on this planet, what is your secret?" In this way I did make a disclosure but did not have a long discussion about my kids instead I focused on the communality of parenting. Again, a small disclosure to show I too am a human being but then I returned with a question about them and their reality. In truth there are a lot of different styles: Virginia Satir was famous for her hugs, she had her hands on people from the get go. You have to decide what you are comfortable with. Again I am not suggesting you share personal details or struggles – good boundaries are essential, but I am suggesting you talk about the weather, you talk about a community tragedy, or if a person comes in with a Yankee cap on you talk about baseball and how you like the Yankees too. I am direct with the people I work with that they are important to me, that it is an honor for me to work with them. I think it is essential that the people we work with feel that we are in the room with them, that they can tell us anything and that they are important to us. So I want to see report cards and I am honored when I get a school picture of one of the kiddos I am working with and it is a super privilege when I get to do some work in a person's home. I do tell people I am proud of them as well as hold shame as tenderly as I can. The "evidence" that I have for being real with the people I work with is when they come to see me ready to do tough work. I work with two folks currently who are challenged with cutting, so much so that cutting has become a regular part of their daily lives. We have gotten to the place where both will show me their arms without being asked to start our time together. This involves a disclosure on their parts as they wear long shelves to avoid people staring or asking questions. When we engage with enough intensity so that our own personality is in the room to enough extent that the people we are working with feel that they are important to us, that we are not "doing therapy on them", rather are walking with them to help them get where they would prefer to be, then we are being real to them. In sum, I offer no critique of psychoanalysis and I do believe in good boundaries, I simply suggest that people seek to engage with a real person, be that person. Below is not a commercial, it is the "real thing".

NB: The four engagement chapters are informed by all the people I have ever worked with, my supervisors as well as the following:

Madsen, W. (2007). Collaborative Therapy with Multi-Stressed Families. NY: Guilford.

Miley, K., O'Melia, M. & DuBois, B. (2009). Generalist Social work practice: An Empowering Approach. Boston: Pearson.

Shulman, L. (1984). The Skills of Helping: Individuals and Groups. Itasca, IL: F.E. Peacock.

Zastrow, C. (1999). The practice of Social Work. Pacific Grove: Brooks/Cole.

Tugboats not plumbers

This is a chapter about orientation to our work. The short of it is to suggest that social workers are like tug boats not like plumbers. I had the pleasure of living in New York City for a good number of years, much of it on the Lower East Side of Manhattan. There I got to watch to watch the tug boats working the East River.

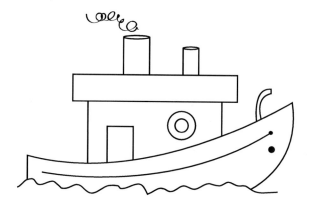

For those in the know, the East River is not exactly a river but a tidal straight-when we get into diversity, we can cover the importance of correct names©. In any event, I grew to love watching what tugs do and what they don't do. The captains of the big boats still have to steer their ships. It is the job to the tug to nudge, push, pull, and to try to be useful in keeping the ship off of the rocks, shoals and other dangers that lurk out there in the swirling tides. I grew to enjoy how the tugs are built to stand tall with the ship they are working with. This reminded me of the concept of "appreciative ally" that Bill Madsen (2007) so often talks about. This appreciative ally stance is about the way in which we can come to know and give credit for the journey that others are on. To be interested how they have fared, how they have made it through the challenging seas that life presents them. It is also about standing with people today in what they face, giving them credit for getting up and addressing themselves to the challenges. The idea being that we can convey to them that we are interested in standing with them against the obstacles. In all these ways we are like tug boats. It is about a core orientation to what we think our role is. We can look at the people we work with as people who are doing the best they can but face more challenges then they can navigate in a way they would prefer to and instead have taken them on a different course that too often has them scraping on the rocks of life. Not lost on me is the fact that tugs have big strong engines, but they are hidden. The engines are below the surface, they are meant to go and go but not race or be showy. Tug boats are workers, rarely are they flashy, they just possess the tools that are needed to be useful in trying to keep folks on course.

This stands in opposition to the plumber. Listen plumbers are essential. There is a saying that "water is the enemy of all architecture". Plumbers are vital, if you have a leak, call one and they can fix it. They keep the leaks from ruining everything. You call a plumber to fix leaks.

While our training and experience often probably does provide us with the ability to fix the challenges that face the people we work with, ultimately that is dis-empowering. That said, please know that the line between being empowering and being dis-empowering is far from being clear. There are times when some "hurdle help"- where you help get a person over a hurdle, acknowledging what you are doing so and then actively offer support for the next hurdle until they can do it easily by themselves is empowering work, especially if you are verbal about what you are doing.

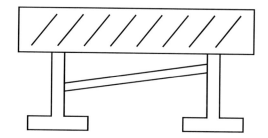

It is good practice to have conversation about the dilemma of enablement verses empowerment. "I HEAR YOU ASKING ME TO DO xxx, AND I COULD, I WORRY THOUGH THAT WHEN I DO SOMETHING THAT YOU COULD DO, I ROB YOU OF THE SATISFACTION YOU GET WHEN YOU DOSOMETHING HARD AND GET IT DONE". This is a "make the process be the content" type of conversation. It is important to be transparent this way so people do not think that you are unwilling to help them, rather you take a stand that at times, not doing for them is more helpful in the long run than doing for them. As we have discussed, we should expect people to be wary of us and of our intentions towards them. They wonder if we really care, we are, after all, being paid. Maybe we are doing it just for money. It might make sense for a person to decide that if I am not willing to do something for them, that I don't like them, don't care or simply don't want to. A conclusion such as this would certainly be counterproductive. In this way I encourage you to be direct and talk it out. This gives you a chance to delve into what your role is and how you try to be useful to people and your belief that they can do it, that you are temporary in their lives, so you cannot fix things, only they can fix things. To be honest, I have had people after I did all that say, "yeah ok, but they listen to you, they don't listen to me, please do it" In situations like that I usually do it, acknowledging that we do not live in affair world but that I believe that they can do it and that ultimately they will have to do it. Clearly this is not a clear path; having a mindset that you are a tugboat not a plumber helps me to navigate the murky boundaries in our work. In the end this whole thing proceeds from believing "I don't fix leaks", I work to empower people so that they can actualize the power that they intrinsically have in them that often is not being brought to bear. In this way I am a tug boat working in the cloudy swirling waters, trying to be useful so folks can fix their own leaks that have sprung upon them.

The Value of your Guts

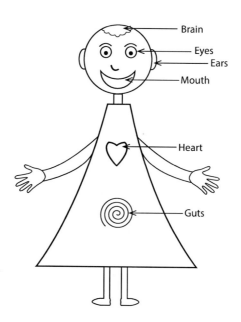

So this chapter is built around a quiz- don't freak out, there is no grade. Look at the drawing of the social worker at the top of the page (the social worker is a female, because most social workers are female). Now imagine that you have been dropped onto an island full of people who need social work services AND you can only bring ONE of these personal attributes: Your **Brain**- your brain is useful for you to think, it remembers all the theory that you have learned so that you can make sense of and understand the people you work with, it is your thinking center. Your **Eyes** – your eyes allow you to observe all that is to be seen, the unsaid emotion, the way people sit next to each other, the condition of the home. The eyes have been called the "windows of the soul" and you can use your eyes to reflect emotion back to people. Your eyes are your observatory center of your practice. Your **Ears**- your ears our are listening appendage, they allow us to hear all that the person is saying to us. The social work profession has been built around listening and we use our ears to do so. Your **Mouth**- your mouth is used to ask questions, to make empathic comments, to offer support, it is our main communication tool. Your **Heart**- the heart is used to feel. We use our heart to connect to the people, to their struggles, their hopes and dreams. We can think of our heart as the emotional center of our practice. Or your **Guts**. By guts, I mean both your intuition and your ability to tolerate. Social workers use their intuition to tune into the vibration that happens between people who are connected. Hard to fully scientifically prove, there is growing evidence of intuition and the more you listen to the gut, the stronger the signal. Guts also are required to handle some of the very difficult material that social workers are asked to work with.

So if you could chose only one of these which would it be _____and how come?_____

_____

There is not wrong answer and clearly we need all of these appendages and the related skill sets that come with them if we can hope to do our best to be useful to people. As the title of this chapter suggests, the author would chose guts. Social workers ask questions that other people just do not ask, but very much need to be asked, and we have to handle the answer. No one wants to ask a five year old girl "has your daddy put his penis in your vagina?" and no one wants to hear that five year old girl say "yes" but we have to be able to ask that question and we have to be able to sensitively handle when the answer comes back as "yes". Asking tough questions, going into homes where domestic violence is a member, or going into homes where there is not an adequate environment for human beings to safely live, comes at a cost: We need to develop a toughness so we can do the job we have been trained to do. That takes guts. Let's face it, the work is hard. It is emotionally draining, and at times physically draining. It takes commitment. Being honest the pressure on us to perform, to achieve positive outcomes will only increase and this will add to the pressure. We need to be able to stay focused on the work. Not staying focused on the work can lead to "alligator arms".

Alligator arms is where we do not fully reach out and grab onto the work. Again no one wants to ask these questions, go to these places, but it is our duty to do so. So if I can have only one, I chose the guts I need to do this job right.

The Code

NASW

This will be a shorter chapter. The message is simple: Use the code (NASW, 2008). The code of ethics is at play every single day you work as a social worker. It is designed to help you out all through the day. It gives you a framework around which to make decisions. If you can develop a quick mental check off "what are my ethical considerations?" when faced with decisions, you will always practice within the code and enjoy a long and fruitful professional life. Society is becoming increasingly complicated; as such, the stickiest part of work has to do with boundaries. All parts of the code are important and all can are associated with ethical challenges but the challenges in a modern society related to boundaries are perhaps the most complex. This point of view comes from spending 18 years on my state's NASW ethics board and seeing the types of cases that have come before the board. Far and away, they have related to boundaries. So listen, repeat after me (out loud!) "I will never have sex with anyone I work with as a social worker, supervisor or teach". See now don't you feel better? That pledge you just made is critical. I have actually heard a case where a person terminated with a person one day and went on a date with their spouse the next day and thought it was ethically ok- nope, nope, nope. See every time a social worker breaks the code, it hurts us all. Since the larger world does not really understand what we do, and movies and TV depict us in a very narrow, often not so flattering light, real life stories of social workers having bad boundaries does hurt the whole profession. It is our job to recognize the multiple boundaries at play in every interaction. We talked some before about simple and basic disclosure as a way to promote engagement, while always being mindful of the boundary to not share too much or have it be too personal and to always have the disclosure lead back to the work. Having worked with kids in care for the past 33 years, I have repeatedly seen what happens when family does not remember a birthday or no one wants the kid for Christmas or Thanksgiving. In these moments I want you to fight the urge to fix the situation, because in reality you can't. I ask you instead to sit with the sadness or the sense of rejection without crossing the boundary of taking the kid home with you. Be close with the people you work with, but don't invite them over for dinner. If you have a romantic feeling for someone, recognize it, talk it out in supervision or your own therapy but do not act on it. The purpose of the boundary is so that the person is safe enough in the relationship to have the space to do the difficult work that they need to do so they can live the way they prefer.

Admittedly, social workers practicing in smaller rural areas have a harder job with boundaries. Small town life means that you cannot be anonymous. A former student of mine grew up in a small town where her family ran the social outlet in the town- the bowling alley. Everyone knew her- she had grown up in the bowling alley and then worked in the bowling alley, now faced with the prospect of working a social worker in the town, made it really tough, because relationships would have to change. In these cases I encourage you to just be very transparent; again this is "process be the content" stuff. Directly have conversations with people where you can tell that you are not being rude, just protecting everyone, so that their business stays private so they can get done what they came to get done.

The other two common areas where I have seen social workers have a challenging time consistently practicing within the code have to do with termination and the challenge of being directed by a supervisor to do something that is not in line with the code. With regard to termination, the code is clear, we cannot drop people. They can drop us, but we are ethically bond to properly terminate, including offering referrals. I have definitely said, more than once "I understand you are not happy with the service, I regret that and understand that because of your experience that you do not think you would ever use such services again, but in case you change your mind, here are three solid options for you". In terms of actual work, coming up with a few referrals often is not the difficult part. The difficult part comes when we are in the midst of a challenging transition. Maybe you have put all of yourself into a situation only to be told to go away. Of course you are going to have some feelings about that. You are not a robot, use supervision to process them out. I would ask you to consider that behind the challenges for so many of the people we work with are issues of loss, that we should expect that transitions are going to be tough. That people who have been left too often, may try to leave before they get left. Try to not see situations such as this a personal condemnation of your practice. At the very least send a letter with three referrals. In this way you have attended to the requirements of good termination practice and perhaps given the person a real avenue to finish what they have started with you.

The situation of being told to do something against the code by your supervisor or a person with some form of power over you is clearly a difficult spot to be in. For the record, the code is clear: The code trumps the supervisor. In practice of course this is challenging as no one wants to be fired for insubordination. Here then is my suggestion: I encourage you to directly share the dilemma and ask the supervisor to help you with it. The type of language I am suggesting would go something like this "OK I am going to need your help, first I need you to know that I value my job and I understand what it means to be insubordinate and have no interest in doing so. At the same time, the directive you gave me seems to be in conflict with the NASW Code of Ethics as I understand it, specifically section xxx, can you help me with this because I am struggling with what I see as an ethical dilemma". Will this work every time? No it will not, but you will have gone on record with your concern. At the end of the day, do the right thing, the right thing is in the code. In practice this has been especially challenging when discharge planning is a part of your job function and you work as part of a interdisciplinary team. Not all professions have a Code of Ethics, or understand the Code you practice under. Respectfully educate others and openly discuss the dilemma. Consistently let people know that you like and understand your job and that you know that you are not one of those people that cannot be a team player, but you need their help because your license and reputation are on the line.

This chapter is directly informed by the Code and the excellent work of Fred Reamer.

National Association of Social Workers (2008). *NASW Code of Ethics*. Washington, DC: Author

Reamer, F. (1998) *Ethical Standards in Social Work*. Washington, DC: NASW Press.

Social work in a post-modern/ socially constructed world AKA Pluto is a planet

10 Chapter

Dear readers do not get scarred but we need to briefly talk philosophy. As an aside I remember my first philosophy class in college; 8am in the morning, in a large lecture hall. This was back in the day when you could smoke in class and the instructor chained smoked throughout, lighting the new one off the butt of the old. If you made the mistake of trying to argue a point, he spent five minutes telling you that you were an idiot. Good times, my only "D" in college. So let's hope this goes over a little better, specifically if the content can be directly related to social work practice. So here goes: Modernism informs us that things are knowable. This then is a drawing of a pencil

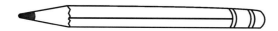

and this is a drawing of a box of tissue.

They are seen as fundamental truths. The world is full of fundamental truths from this philosophy. Post-modernism has become more in-vogue in recent years. Post-modernism takes a different tact. Post-modernism says that truths are socially constructed. So this is only a pencil because we decided to call it a pencil, we could have called it a "box of tissue" and that would have been our truth. That there is nothing about it that really makes it a pencil, it is just that we have decided to call it a pencil. Here is a story to further illustrate. When my children were younger, parents were required to teach Sunday school every other year in order for the kids to go to the Sunday school at the religious organization we belonged to at the time. I was paired with a professor of Astrophysics from the large, very prestigious University in town as the two teachers for the kiddos. As much as I try to form successful relationships with everyone, our first meeting had not gone well, and I was worried about being a teaching team with a person I struggled to communicate with. Then there was big news; scientists had decided that Pluto was not a planet but was a sphere – I figured we could chat about this new scientific fact as it was in his area of interest and that could help us bond. So the next week, I said "so what do you think about the news that Pluto is now a ..." I didn't finish the sentence as he slapped his hands right in my face and pronounced "Pluto is definitely a sphere!" Well my hope of us have a dialogue about the new fact had not worked so I needed to try another approach to make a working relationship with this fellow. But I thought about the scientific question more and more, this is what I came to: Pluto had always been a planet in my world. See in my world there are nine planets, with Pluto being the little cute one at the end. Then I thought that it does not really matter if I keep thinking that Pluto is a planet- no doubt the scientist has a great reason why it does not rate planet status, but to me, in my world, it is, has been a planet. So I decided that I will continue to view Pluto as a planet and in fact most likely always will view Pluto as a planet. That is social constructionism. How people put the world together is the "truth". This not to say that there are no other truths, from a social constructionist perspective there most certainly are, that is not the point. The point is to ask ourselves, "what is the truth of the person we are working with?" As social workers our job is to accept the truth of the people we work with. There are a lot of advantages this philosophy can give us. For one thing it can help us to not put too much stock in our own formulations. I am not saying they are not correct; I am willing to bet that you are correct in your formulation. What I am suggesting is that for the most part, unless the person we are working with can see the formulation in a way similar to the way you do, it will not be useful to them. The easiest example is diagnosis. Whether you use the ICD-10 or DSM 5, through training and experience you will get to the place that your diagnostic skill is spot on. This is important, with proper diagnosis, there are better, more evidenced based treatments. There are things I do with folks that are faced with Generalized Anxiety Disorder, which I do not do with those that have to deal with Paranoid Schizophrenia on a daily basis. At the same time when making a diagnosis, I do it with a person and I start with the question "part of coming here (to the mental health clinic I work at) is that we need to have a diagnosis for billing purposes, I don't know if you have thought about this before, but if you had to, what diagnosis for yourself would you chose?". To me this is respectful and relates back to our conversation about respect. Deeper than that, the minute that I, a White man with a PhD tells someone they have a diagnosis, I have assigned a truth, and by doing so have shaped a reality. I am contributing to how the reality is constructed; in this case very much in the social exchange I am having with the person. That is more power than I am completely comfortable with. I am not saying I am not right in my diagnosis; I tend to believe in my skill in this area, what I am saying is that the process by which I assign a truth to another person is loaded and we need to be very careful about the impact of our imparting truths on others. We can get more into the power of labels in the future, but for now, please chew on the question of how you put things together. Really there is no right or wrong on this one- modernist or post-modernist, just think about where the "truth" comes from. Most importantly consider the effect of the truth coming from you has on the person you are working with. Finally to ask yourself, be real honest with yourself about the intersection of assigning truth with your ideas about your practice as a social worker.

I want to acknowledge again that this is a heavy chapter. In no way should this be read as any kind of diminishment of your knowledge and skill. People come to you precisely because you have that knowledge and skill. They expect you to have that knowledge and skill. Being confident in your knowledge and skill is required for you to do well in practice. The question is about are you aware of the power of our truths on the person we work with. As an example, let's take the basic case record of any kid and family I have ever worked with. Usually the worse five minutes of their life are recorded over and over with ascribing of intention and a lot of labels. These labels have power and they tend to follow people around. From a social construction mindset, sooner or later, the person often starts to believe in the truth of the label enough that they act consistently with the label. This is an example of the "truth" doing the person. Here is a personal story. When I was around eight or nine, my buddy and I started a small fire inside a metal trash can next to his wooden garage. Then we each got a container of lighter fluid, climbed up on the roof of the wooden garage to see if we could squirt the lighter fluid into the fire and see how high a flame we could get. From a Darwinian perspective, no doubt we were nearing the extinction of our lives when my buddy's step father came around the corner. While he was enraged, he put the fire out and no damage was done. We were able to go about our lives (my buddy is a successful mechanical engineer making heart values in Australia) without label. However I have met many youth who were not so lucky, their record says "FIRE STARTER" all over it, and it does significantly affect the way people look at them and the kind of services they do and do not offer them. The point of all this is to try to hold our truths as lightly as possible, maybe that a billions year old rock way out in space does not care what people call it, but the folks we work with actually do care what we call them.

Growing Grass

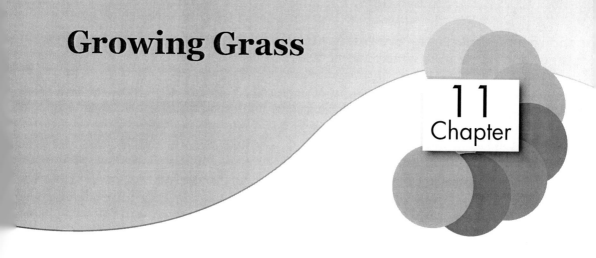

This chapter starts with a picture of yours truly mowing his lawn. As of the writing of this book, I have lived in the same house for 17 years. The house sits at the edge of a midsized city called Rochester in upstate New York. Similar to a lot of parts of America, we are obsessed with grass. There is some unspoken connection to having a green lawn that just signals success. This is one of those socially constructed things: having a green lawn full of grass means you are successful. Because it is America there are a lot of products out there to help you get that "look". The thing of it is, when you look at what is in those bags of stuff to put on your lawn it is full of all kinds of dangerous chemicals designed to kill non grass growing things and stimulate grass growing. Now I myself actually really dislike dandelions. I have this little hand tool

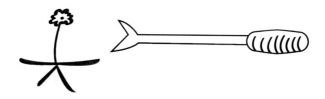

that I use to dig them out. I walk around the yard once a week or so and pop out the dandelions. What I don't do is put down harmful chemicals. Actually I never have, not once. There is a method, it is called "overseeding" where you spread grass seed on top of grass and water it. See all grass needs to grow is water, if you want more grass, put down more grass seed and water it. It is directly a response to the question "what do you want?" Well if you want grass, grass seed and water will do the trick, again if something you don't want comes up, you can individually remove it. As social workers we often are presented with situations and are told about somebody's bad behavior with the hope that we have some bag of lawn treatment that can make it go away. I am directly suggesting that you ask the referring party "what do you want Johnny to do?" then ask "when was the last time he did that?" and then get real curious about what was happening when he was doing what people wanted him to do. See I don't really know how to stop Johnny from throwing chairs in class, but I do believe that I can be useful in getting him to do his math. So here comes one of those really big things from this book, I will put it in bold so you don't miss it: **Problems and solutions are not necessarily connected.** This is a Bill Madsen idea. Simple sentence, big idea. I really question why it makes sense to put down all these harmful chemicals to grow grass. Those chemicals are bad for the neighborhood dogs, the birds, little children, and our water supply. Let's be about what we want to have happen and go about making that happen. When people come to see you, be respectful, get to know the challenges in their lives, but be more interested in the solution. Another example, I have tons of years of experience working with high risk youth. That means I have had tons of kids who smoke weed and other people who want them to stop. You may not agree with this, but go find some 16 year old that is getting high and ask them to stop. Were you effective? See youth will stop when they want to. I am not saying that marijuana is good for human beings in general or developing youth in particular, but I am saying that there is a lot of activity aimed at changing behavior that does not use good motivational strategy to get people to change their behavior. What I suggest is that you start by finding out what they do outside of the weed, which can lead to a conversation about the weed controlling them maybe that can open a door, just telling people to change their behavior, even under duress rarely changes behavior. Separating people and the challenges they face is one critical piece, the other is finding out where people want to go. This gets us out of the plumbing business and into the hopes and dreams business. Perhaps you are skeptical, so here is the deal, I live in Rochester, NY. If you will be in my neck of the woods, send me an e-mail and I'll have you over for a grass tour, we can look at my lawn and look at the lawn of my neighbors. I have good neighbors but a large number of them put down chemicals, I know because the lawn chemical companies are required by law to put up these little plastic signs telling people to not let their dogs or young children on the yard for a couple days until the toxins are a "safe" level. I ask you to compare lawns, mine has been chemical free for at least 17 years, and I have green grass too. This is because I want to have green grass and I go about making green grass happen, not attack the problem, I make the solution happen. The take home here is for us to be about helping people be and do want they aspire to do, not what they don't. Let me close with the easy example: "I want to lose ten pounds". My response "what is it that you are going for?" They say again "I want to lose ten pounds". So again I have to ask them, what they want, and then you will hear about looking better, feeling better, being more active, and being more attractive. Once you have what they want you can go after that. You can explore when was the last time they felt more active or more attractive and what was happening for them then. By linking what people want to times when it already happens, shows a pathway to have it happening more. That way we avoid the trap of failing to stop a negative.

Madsen, W. (2007). *Collaborative Therapy with Multi-Stressed Families.* NY,NY: Guilford.

Externalization

Picking up on a concept that we referred to but did not name in the growing grass chapter, we need to briefly discuss externalization. All credit must be given to the two Narrative Therapy guru's: David Epston and Michael White for the development of this exciting and useful therapeutic tool. I encourage you to explore their writings on this subject and their therapeutic approach in general. Recall the central idea in the "growing grass" chapter asked us to think about what we would like people to do, not what we would like them not to do. The truth is that the problems or challenges in people's lives do carry a lot of weight and it is inappropriate to not address those challenges on some level. Again we are not in the fixing problems business but we do need to appreciate the power of the problem/challenge. One of the ways that problems/challenges exert their power is by their association to the person. If we are being honest, those of us in the helping professions have to shoulder some responsibility here. The process of diagnosis has left a lot of people walking around dragging a label.

Especially when working with people who have had contact with the helping profession for some time, they spit their diagnosis back at us as they are accepted facts "I'm bipolar", "my anxiety disorder…", "I'm just depressed" and so forth. I have come to found these self-descriptions distressing and that is what led me to the Collaborative therapy of Bill Madsen or the Narrative therapy movement. See it no longer matters if the person is bipolar, has an anxiety or depressive disorder, if they think they do, they will respond in a manner consistent with that label and will drag it around and unwittingly dredge it up at the most inopportune times. The disorder has become a part of the person so they get up in the morning, put on their socks, underwear, bipolar, shirt, anxiety, slacks – you get the idea. Michael White and David Epson invented a technique to create some space called externalization. The heart of the idea is to use language to show the person that they are in relationship with the challenges in their life but they themselves are not the challenge. When I am working I will often demonstrate this idea by pulling two chairs together and have the person sit in one chair and then tell them that they are a beautiful fantastic, special and unique human being who has a special relationship with the thing that is in the chair next to them. Then we work together to give that thing a name, for instance we can call that thing "depression", the name should come from the person if at all possible, but most importantly we should stress that it is definitely separate from them. Again, as much as possible have them name it, the more the "it" is in their words not our words, the more it will be meaningful to them. Not to turn this into an English lesson, but the idea is to take an adjective and make it a noun so "I'm anxious" becomes "the anxiety".

From a technique approach narrative minded therapists will then use some semi-scripted questions to discuss the nature of the now externalized problem. They would liken this to the metal scaffolding put around an older building that is getting a face lift so to speak. For instance, I discuss with the person the ways in which "the depression" has an effect on their life. We would explore the specific things that "depression" can get you to do. I ask about any special tricks "depression" has up its sleeve to get you to follow "depression". The idea here is to flesh out , via a conversation the story that the problem has built so that you can then deconstruct it, expose it and looks for cracks in the problem story. The thinking here is that in many situations the problem story has become so big and powerful that it obscures all the other stories that are going on in a person's life. Problems are just like that, they often are louder than the things that are going well for a person. Bill Madsen often points out that we need to have good ears for the competency that is present as it can be drowned out by the problem noise. Once we have deconstructed the problem, we can inquire about the stories that are not as loud, where the person has ignored, outwitted or gone around the problem. The times where there were exceptions to the rule. The times where the person lived as they would prefer and then start to get real curious how they made that happen and to explore the meaning behind how they made what they want happen. In this way externalization becomes even more than a powerful tool, it becomes the way we work. Interestingly, as we will discuss more in subsequent chapters, asking questions this way makes engagement, assessment and intervention a simultaneous process rather than three distinct parts of practice and this has numerous advantages, especially with regard to our practice feel like we are working with rather than working on a person or family.

White, M. & Epson, D. (1990). *Narrative Means to Therapeutic Ends*. NY: Norton.

Can anyone tell me what time it is?

A discussion of time zones

For those of you not well versed in classic rock music, one gift from the late 1960's was the band *Chicago*, whose horn driven sound led to a number of hits including the title of this chapter. Time is an important thing to consider as all psychological theory is organized around time. As far as we know, there are only three time zones: there is the past, the present and the future. The field of psychology began as a study of the past. Freud and his followers use analysis to understand the past. The patient talked, the therapist listened and offered interpretation of how the past is played out in functioning of the drives, the Id, Ego and Superego. Later Ego psychologists as well as Bowen family therapy explore history to look for patterns that continue to play out today. The genogram is an excellent tool for tracing the patterns that repeat in families over the generations. This is solid, well established practice and has shown to be effective.

Speaking of effective, there are several, well studied approaches that focus on the present time zone. Salvador Minuchin developed *Structural Family Therapy* as a way to work with family power, alignment and boundaries in the present and make change to promote a more healthy family structure and thereby functioning. Most well-known of all is the collection of therapies that fall under the social learning category. Here we are talking about, *Cognitive therapy, Behavioral therapy, Cognitive-Behavioral therapy* and more recent applications such as *Trauma-Focused Cognitive Behavioral therapy.* The studying of these approaches has found them t⌐

be the most evidenced based approaches in our field and are successful for a great number of people. In general, when working in some of these present-time framed focused therapies, the therapist works to understand the environment so to speak around a behavior (antecedents, triggers and so forth) and sets up an intervention.

The future though is only one of the three time zones where we have the possibility of something different than what happened in the past or is happening today, can actually happen. As much as people come to see social worker so that things can be different, the only place where things can actually be different is in the future. This is not to knock past or present-based practice interventions, clearly they are effective, at the same time it is important to point out where possibility lives. Possibility lives in the future. Let us consider a metaphor. Life has often been metaphorically described as the process of going down a road. Here is my drawing of a road.

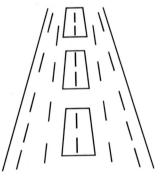

I want to challenge that metaphor. See if you are going down a road, you can turn around and go back. In life however, at least so far, science has not enabled us to really go back. Sure you can move back to your home town, or you can get back together with a former love interest but things are not the same- not saying that those are not good activities to do but things are not the same. Perhaps life is more like skiing down a hill.

Can anyone tell me what time it is? A discussion of time

39

Here the force of gravity propels you down the mountain, you cannot go back. You can stop, but sooner or later, you are going to get cold, so you turn your ski's and down you go. While traveling down you can turn some to avoid bumps, but that takes practice and skill and fresh legs. When the slope gets too steep, or we go too fast or are tired, we may fall. Life seems like skiing. As such the only place we can do anything about is the path in front of us. This then is a plug for the value of *Solution-Focused, Narrative and Collaborative* therapy. All of these approaches believe that the one place people can be different is in the future, because the future has not happened yet, the possibility for being different, for change are limitless. All use possibility as a motivational asset in the work. By using technique to uncover existing assets that are being buried or ignored by the weight or focus of the challenge, we can help people move in their preferred direction. This becomes a motivating and exciting way to work. That being said we need to be very clear in our own minds where the challenges really are and that is the focus of the next chapter.

This chapter has referenced a number of therapies, for more information on them the reader is directed to go:

Beck, A. (1976). *Cognitive Therapy and the Emotional Disorders*. Meridian: NY.

Cohen, J., Mannarino, A. & Deblinger, E. ((2006). *Treating Trauma and Traumatic Grief in Children and Adolescents*. Guilford: NY.

Freud, S. (1938). *The Basic Writings of Sigmund Freud*. Random House: NY.

Madsen, W. (2007). *Collaborative Therapy with Multi-Stressed Families*. NY,NY: Guilford.

Minuchin, S. & Fishman, H. C. (1981). *Family Therapy Techniques*. Harvard University Press: Cambridge, MA.

Madsen, W. (2007). *Collaborative Therapy with Multi-Stressed Families*. NY,NY: Guilford.

Where the problem really is

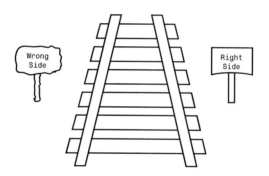

This is a drawing of a railroad track with a right side and an other side of the tracks.. This chapter is centered on a discussion of where problems lie. The thesis of this chapter is that too much of the information coming at the people we work with has left them with the inescapable conclusion that they are the problem. The things that family, friends, teachers, social workers and others have said to them reinforce the idea that they are the source of their problems. The whole process of diagnosis results in a diagnostic label that clearly is seen by many as a personal deficit. The way that mental health challenges are portrayed and discussed in the print, visual and electronic media contributes to the notion that problems live in the person, that they are the fault of the person. The individual mindset so prevalent in Western world culture contributes to the idea that people and their problems go hand in hand. This idea that a person is from "the other side of the tracks" reinforces that people and their problems are one and the same. In the city where I live and work, we have a "Fatal Crescent" drawn here.

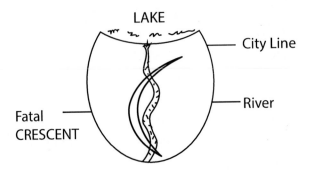

LAKE

City Line

River

Fatal
CRESCENT

We are told that inside that crescent are most of the murders, rapists, crack whores, prostitutes, gangs, violence and so forth. This in reality is the politics of fear playing the blame and shame game. This is a political comment but it seems that our system demands that there be an "other side of the tracks". If we are being really honest this blame game is harder on women, on people of color, the LGBTQ community, the poor and children/youth. One unearned privilege that us white men get is a lot of leeway with regard to our own challenges. The lack of this leeway that just is not equally granted then seems to get internalized as self-deficit. As discussed back in the chapter about the Planet Pluto, the "truth" is a moving target. In fact there are many truths out there. A very real issue is that the process of communicating those truths to others often has an negative effect on them. As people we are vulnerable to these truths coming at us. Tell me I look nice to today and I think I look nice, tell me I am a "crazy B" and I think less of myself. When the labels get concentrated they gain power. So for people who live "across the tracks" or in the "fatal crescent", many internalize that truth, and then that internalization becomes a force. The thesis of this chapter is to move the thinking so that the problem is the problem, that people are not the problem. Here is a list of problems: Poverty, domestic violence, high levels of lead in homes, HIV/AIDS, homelessness, poor performing schools, the lack of local jobs, neighborhoods with environmental pollution, substance abuse, and mental illness. Those are problems, people are not problems, but they live in relationship to those problems.

Our job is to help people gain some perspective. When we can separate people from their problems, we help them gain that perspective. One way to do this is to externalize the problem from the person. We talked about this in chapter 12, once we have externalized the problem from the person, we need to get real curious about the times that they stand in opposition to the problem. I work with a beautiful 18 year old woman who has survived a harrowing history of neglect and abuse. Along the way she learned to cut and cut and cut. Rows of half inch long cuts line her arms and legs. Recently she caught her boyfriend cheating on her. That voice inside her said "there is something wrong with you, that is why you are not enough for him" and she began to cut, but she stopped and became angry, she described a new thought, "wait I was committed and loyal, I did give my emotion freely, maybe it is he not me who is less worthy". The work in session was to explore that movement away from, in opposition to, the repeated theme of rejection and pain, to one of purpose. In short, to move the story of the problem from inside to outside, including the idea that the boyfriend may also be influenced by a young male culture that looks at fidelity as a sign of weakness and lack of male prowess.

All this is not to diminish that there are very real challenges that people face; schizophrenia, domestic violence, incest, substance abuse are real. The point is that those things are the problem; the person you are working with is ensnarled in a relationship with those challenges, one of our key functions is to help people see the relationship they are in with the challenges and to see those times in which they live outside of the pull or influence of those problems. In addition, it is vital that as people who have gained the privilege of making a DSM 5 or ICD-10 diagnosis, that we consider the implications of the diagnostic process. The suggestion here is that we approach the subject of diagnosis from a partner perspective as much as possible. I say to the people I am working with "coming here requires that we have a diagnosis, do you have a diagnosis that makes sense to you" then we go about discussing the diagnosis from a number of angles to try to mitigate the effect of the diagnosis on the person. Truth is if all things were equal, I am willing to bet that most folks would rather live on the "right" side of the tracks; it is just that the forces outside of them make it difficult to do so today. This translates in our work to two interrelated ideas: First can we separate people from the real challenges they face so they can have the space to actually work on living the life they would prefer. Second, can we work in such a way so that we do not reinforce the belief system that they are the problem? This is not to say that we do not need to challenge unhealthy behavioral choices, because we do need to challenge unhealthy behavior choices, I am suggesting we do so in a respectful manner communicating "you are more than what you do- you are a person with hopes, dreams and aspirations, just like everyone else".

Assessment

Following engagement, assessment is usually the next practice skill that we learn in social work school. A quick and easy definition of assessment is that assessment is a way to think about something. As practitioners this practice skill is best seen as an evolving process. As all human beings, families, groups, organizations and communities are in constant motion and change, so to should our assessments move with them. In this way it is similar to an evergreen tree, hence the drawing of an evergreen tree.

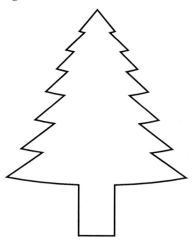

Assessment has several interrelated purposes: At the most basic level we use assessment as a way to understand. Assessment provides a frame to view and organize our understandings. Ideally this coming to an understanding is a collaborative process, a joint venture in understanding. We also use assessment as a planning tool. In this way assessment becomes a helpful guide of where to go and perhaps in what order we will work together to address the challenges. Again, when approached as a collaborative process, having a mutual understanding about where we are going makes the work be more focused. A third way that we as social workers use assessment is to identify needed supports, or resources and to identify the strengths that are already in place. This is to directly encourage us all to assess as widely as possible, if we believe that the solution is already present, then we need to make sure that our process helps to illuminate it. Clearly many folks use assessment to make a diagnosis. Related to the discussion in the previous chapter, it is important to acknowledge that the model that we have inside of us does influence how we make assessment and what we see. Ego psychologists assess the ego and its functions. Narrative minded clinicians assess the stories that emerge. One important consideration with respect to assessment is to be mindful that all of us assess based on how we think the challenges in people's lives come about. It really is important to take a step back and ask yourself how do problems happen? We live in a time where the acceptable political rhetoric is filled with blame; this undoubtedly has an influence on us all. Assessment is influenced by gender, class, race, ethnicity, spiritual belief, age and many other important attributes of both the person doing the assessment and the person(s) being assessed. While training can reduce the influence of these important factors, to deny them is to shortchange the other person and yourself. Work to be as objective as possible but acknowledge that there are limits to objectivity. You can work on objectivity by asking yourself, "What am I taking for granted? What assumptions am I making? What conclusions are I making based on those assumptions?" This is critical, clearly what we see, what models we believe in, will dictate how we go about working to make change.

It is also well known that social workers are famous for using tools to make assessment. Yes observation, active listening, and asking good curious questions go a long way, but we are also skilled at using genograms, ecomaps, force field analysis and other visual assessment aids in the process. Gaining familiarity with these tools before using them seem natural and unforced. To the extent possible, try to share a copy of anything you have done, many families I have had the honor of working with enjoy their genograms as a visual representation of their history. A special mention needs to made here for the value of going to the place where people live. The home visit is a treasure trove. Frankly it is so much easier to assess for strengths in the home, because they are all around you in the photographs, awards, style, cooking and more relaxed atmosphere in most cases than the agency office.

One activity I do in class when teaching about assessment is to give each student a half sheet of industrial grade paper towel, and then make them give me two assessments of the item I gave them that no one else in the class has offered while I write them down on the board. What usually happens is a really interesting list which can be grouped by quality, form, and function. Often there are contradictions (cheap and invaluable or smooth and rough). The point is that if you can fill a white board with assessment of a half sheet of industrial grade paper towel, think about what you could do with a person, family, group, organization or community. Assessment, in conclusion is an evergreen tree, an on-going opportunity for us to be really curious and seek to understand.

McGoldrick, M., Gerson, R., & Shellenberger, S. (1999). Genograms. *Assessment and Intervention. New York: Norton*.

Parker, J., & Bradley, G. (2014). *Social work practice: Assessment, planning, intervention and review*. Learning Matters.

Brager, G., & Holloway, S. (1993). Assessing prospects for organizational change: The uses of force field analysis. *Administration in Social Work, 16*(3-4), 15-28.

Termination practice

Basically without exception, our work with any individual, family, group, organization or community does come to an end. Endings tend to be a difficult time for many of us. As we have discussed, loss is an issue for many of the people we work with. The beauty and opportunity in termination work therefore needs to be attended to. Often times therapeutically more can be accomplished in the final sessions than seem to be happening in the prior work. While I am well aware that the term "corrective emotional experience" has gone out of favor in the clinical world, when well attended to, which is exactly what good termination work can look like. Providing a different kind of ending than the fading away without any processing or worse, sudden departure, that is all too common in the lives of some many people I work with, becomes therapeutic. Ethically we are bound to give notice to people and not dump them. This is important. Even if your boss tells you to get a person out that day, you are ethically bound to do a safe discharge. Even if you decide the relationship is 100% non-therapeutic, you are ethically bound to give referrals to other providers. Even if they fire you, you should offer a referral. Here is a drawing of a "no-boot". You can discharge but you need to at least try to link them with needed services.

As much as possible termination should be planned. In working with younger children, then making a calendar/stick chart is helpful. With older humans, being direct about the importance of a planned last session, and if they will not do that, at least some time spent in a sudden last session to review the work. It is useful for the person to tell us what was useful and what was not useful. You can frame it as a gift they can give the next person we work with. The whole idea is to change the experience with leaving and loss so that they feel good about themselves and ideally have some sense of perspective of where they have come.

Aside from above, what the objective is in termination work is to pull together the work. To help folks gain perspective on where they have come from and how they have gotten to a changed place. It is a time when you can be most real and congratulate them on the hard work and let them know how much it meant to you to see them grow. I directly let folks know what a privilege it has been for me. Work to reinforce the gains by having them tell you how they have done it and how they can continue to do it. Often times the work is not 100% success, so framing change as a process, a journey that they have started on and made progress with is motivating. The termination work is designed to be inspirational for the future, either for more therapeutic work or to just continue in the direction that the person (s) is going.

On Diversity practice

This story will sound like I am throwing stones, I am not, I am telling you a true story that I think illustrates the challenge we continue to have with diversity education, so here goes: I had the great opportunity to teach for a brief period in a social work college in Southern India. One day I was sitting with my good colleague who directs their MSW program and asked her what she was going to teach that afternoon? "I am teaching on diversity" she replied. Interested, I asked what textbook she used. She pulled out a book, that while I do not use, I do know well as it is a leading social work practice text. I opened it to the diversity chapter. It began with content on working with African American families followed by some sections of Latino families from various Caribbean and Central American countries next came working with Asian families followed by a section on working with LGBTQ individuals. I looked at her and asked if this content made any sense to her students, she smiled in an embarrassed way and simply said "no, but it is what we have in the field today". Sadly she is right. Much of what we have implies that the reader is a majority white American reader working with some American minority. As much as we can say the world is small, when it comes to teaching about diversity, we seem so squeezed by racism on the one side and fear of being politically incorrect on the other, that we tend to sanitize or globalize the content so we don't get dirty. In the end it feels to me like there is a collective "let's just through this unharmed" approach.

Well I am here to tell you, that I am a racist. I wish did not have racist thoughts (I am using racist to represent any thought that "others" another human being), but I do. I work hard to address them but they are persistent, subtle and ugly. I had the benefit of having progressive parents, but as we have seen, liberalism has failed to address either systemic racism or othering, and has in fact done a ton of damage in perpetuating multiple forms of diversity challenges. Clearly we have deep and enduring challenges in America with regard to racism and othering. While there are bright spots, our collective inability to practice acceptance of others who are not from the so-called majority culture is a gnawing weakness in our society. It also presents as a real and persistent challenge to every social work practitioner. So what to do?

Start off by working to see the picture as it really is. It does not matter who we elect as president that just is not a sign that we got this. If the solution was that simple we would have done it a long time ago. This work is hard but it is possible to move the pile in the right direction and for you to practice from an increasingly informed perspective. You can start by making a conscious commitment to stay a woke on the fact that we live in a polarized world with a lot of unhealthy belief regarding anyone who looks, acts, believes different from the way do. Here is a drawing of a person waking up. Use it to remind yourself that you gotta stay woke!

Next, the phrase "experience is the best teacher" is true. It is not uncommon in social work school to have an assignment to go and be a minority in a situation and then write some type of reflection paper. That is the idea; it is just that we have to do it repeatedly. Once is good, a 1,000 times is better. The way systemic racism plays out in America is that most people live in a neighborhood with limited diversity. That translates into attending grade schools with limited diversity. Add to this, pretty much all of us spend a good amount of time watch TV and movies where we are bombarded with messages about diversity that leave an imprint on our thinking. Let's return to India for example. India is the world's second largest country. Census data shows a little over 1% of all Americans identify as of Indian descent (over 3 million people), many of whom are in the high tech field. On the screen though they are most often cab drivers and seven-eleven counter workers. Yes there is one comic actor who is well known but one actor, like one president, like one assignment in social work school does not cause change. You need to push yourself. You need regular emersion; a consistent widening of your circle so that you continue to evolve. It may feel like you are pushing a big rock up a mountain. Here is a drawing of Sisyphus pushing that rock up that mountain to remind you of your task.

Another idea is to think about the whole social construction of difference and maybe the fallacy that this house of cards is built upon can motivate you to work for change. If there is any concept that best defines social constructionism, it would be difference. Literally a couple thousand years ago, the belief that in the flat world (these ideas predate us knowing the world is round) there were three kinds of people Caucasoid, Negroid and Mongoloid. We have not evolved much. There was a United States census the year I was born and on it there were only three racial group boxes to check. Now there are more boxes today but we still are about putting people into boxes. It is not just about forms, scientists over the past 2,000 years have been looking to show proof that we are different. Guess what? There is no gene that is in all African Americans and not in Asian Americans, actually there is more genetic difference within African Americans than between African Americans and Caucasian Americans. There is no gene in self-identified homosexual Americans that is not in self-identified straight Americans. We made this whole thing up and applied a lot of thinking behind it. That is social constructionism and it is powerful and it gets in the way of our work.

The truth that I have found for myself is that diversity is always at play when I am working as a social worker. The more I can recognize diversity and practice some form of cultural humility, the more I am open to noticing when diversity between us has walked into our conversations, into our relationships, and the better I am able to do my job. So it is not so much new knowledge that I need (although know is important), what I need to do is positon myself to be a willing and on-going learner. I need to stay humble, but be active in seeking to unpack the suitcases of ideas I have that are not so pretty about others. We do not get to choose who we work with as social workers. Our ability to be successful does require us to have good diversity practice skills.

Family Practice an Introduction

This is a drawing of a family. When you look at it, I want you to remember that everyone has a family. Maybe it is only a whisper or a distant memory but everyone has a family. As social workers we have been trained to understand that families do have a great influence on people as they develop. Most of us were trained to use a systems perspective when thinking about families. Family systems thinking is an American idea. It is a cool story of cross fertilization and discovery. The idea of applying systems thinking to families sprouted in the late 1950's from a group working in Palo Alto, California who were looking at the communication patterns of people suffering from schizophrenia. The leader of the group was a man named Gregory Bateson. The cool part is that in the late 1950's America was obsessed with getting to the moon. We wanted to get there before the Russians, so we needed rocket ships that needed a brain called a computer. The folks working to get us to the moon were systems thinkers. The story goes that the rocket/moon/computer folks visited the same watering holes after work as Bateson and his crew and ideas crossed. Here is a drawing of a rocket ship going to the moon to help you recall the good fortune of applying systems thinking to families.

To continue, families are systems who are comprised of individuals, who are systems in and of themselves. Most important here was the shift from linear thinking to systems thinking. Linear thinking had dominated psychological thought to this point. Basically A > B, now looks like A is influenced by F, R and S which leads to B. So behavior that had traditionally been viewed as pathological and intrapsychic was now considered interpersonal and relational. Shifting from the inner workings of the mind to understanding of relationships in context (basically person in environment) opened the door for family work as a form of practice to be developed.

Families are the building blocks of our species and families seem to have an increasingly hard job as our society speeds up. Thinking about all the societal changes in the past roughly 60 years since Bateson and his group started applying systems thinking to families, one has to appreciate the demands on the American family. For instance we have seen a huge shift in gender roles. Women are a huge part of the workforce, virtually gone is *June Clever* waiting for *Ward* to come home with her apron on as she chases after the *Bev*. Roughly 12 percent of the children in America are raised by a grandparent in a home where neither parent resides. America is increasingly blessed by people from all over the world, who bring their family practices to this country. Gains in granting full rights to gay and transgender people has expanded the definition of what a family is. This evolving story is essential in directing our practice to work with the modern family in America.

As practitioners we need to appreciate the power and intensity of how a family is defined. Clearly membership as a family member does imply all kinds of social rights verses people who would not "count" as family. At the same time, readers of this text are encouraged to adopt the idea is that we should ask who are the members of a family and then take their word. Our job is not be census counters, it is to be useful and no one knows better who "belongs" than the family itself. So many of us have an Aunt who is actually not related but is our Aunt just the same, or have a pet who is as much a member as any person. Some would not consider their biological father a member but their grandmother 20 years deceased as the most important family member today. Now it is your turn; on the rest of the page, draw your family, then take a look at your drawing and ask yourself how who is there, who is not there and how this drawing informs your practice as a family –minded practitioner.

Family practice: Getting started

When systems thinking are applied to a situation, the challenges that are facing a family can now be largely viewed as having an interactive root. The interactive nature of challenges is true for even the more biological challenges such as schizophrenia, where people with schizophrenia show the influence of the interactive piece in the way the disorder manifests itself differently in different environments. Proceeding now with an interactive lens you are ready to begin family work. Family work can be daunting. For the first thing, there are usually more of them than of us. Simply put, you are outnumbered. In addition, whenever possible it is excellent to do family work on their turf. The family home is such a rich place to be. The photos, the knick-knacks and the comfort level of the family members adds much to the clinical encounter. Being in the family home also gives you access to family members who most likely, would never be seen in the office. Those times where I got to meet and talk with the great grandfather who holds the family wisdom, or the gang-affiliated boyfriend of the sister who has great influence on the youth I am working with, has made a huge difference in my own understanding of the work in front of me. I submit that these are the types of understanding that you just do not get in the office.

The next fairly daunting thing about family practice is that there are a number of different schools of family practice. How do you know which one is best? Can you mix and match? To assist in the first question, I have organized the bibliography by content area with some brief notes about the books so that you can explore this subject (and the others) in more depth. As we have talked about time before, time is a variable that has been important in family work. So Bowen's work or the genograms that Monica McGoldrick has brought to us, look to the past. The structural family work of Salvador Minuchin or the conjoint family work of Virginia Satir are very much present focused and the narrative family work of Michael White and David Epston, solution-focused family work of Steve De Shazier and Insoo Kim Berg or the collaborative therapy of Bill Madsen are future based. This is far from a complete list, so further study is required. As for the question of mix and match, most will recommend against it, in general the more a school is pushing for an evidence base for their approach, the more they will be against a mix and match approach. Multisystemic family therapy would be an example of an approach that preaches strict fidelity to the model. That said, every school does offer something, and if you are not bound by a mandate from your employer, it may make good sense to borrow a technique or two and integrate them into your practice. For your own sense of efficacy though, it is good to know where you get things from. So if you see the triangles in a family, know you are using some structural thinking, or if you ask exception questions, you are using a solution focused approach – this will just help you feel more on top of your practice.

Let us dig a little deeper into this last idea by way of an example. Not long after I was promoted to be the supervisor of a kinship foster care unit, my phone rang and on the other end was Jorge Collapinto, one of Minuchin's major disciples. He invited me and my team to bring our kinship families to where he was working so we may train under him and the families could get the benefit of his approach. In this way I got to learn a lot about structural family therapy and I am forever grateful. At the same time, I do not work as a structural family therapist, but I do think that Minuchin's writings on how to join with families are as clear and as useful as anything I have ever read, and I do use them. Minuchin and Fishman (1981) suggest employing some strategies when getting started with families to promote good joining. The first is to train yourself to notice the invisible wires that exist between family members. Notice who always sits next whom, who always agrees with each other, who talks first, who nods their head when another speaks, basically you are asked to follow the process of a conversation. This is called *tracking* and it is a good skill for any of you to use in my mind no matter what school or style of work. Here is a drawing of a puppet on a set of strings to remind you that there are connections between family members.

A second idea that you might find really useful comes to us from Virginia Satir and her *Conjoint Family Therapy* (1967). Yes that is an old citation, but her ideas remain fresh. One in particular has always struck me as relevant and that is that we need to be as knowledgeable about how we connect to others as we are about how we connect to ourselves. Satir said we are not robots going about employing techniques on others, she would say we are "people making" and we cannot do that without awareness. Having self-awareness is vital for all forms of practice but especially so in family work where, as I said there are usually more of them than us. Satir herself was a tougher, a hugger, she had her hands on you from jump street. Others of us prefer not to touch other people. The point is not to be like her or me for that matter, the point is to know how you connect to yourself. How can you reasonably expect to connect to other people if you are not aware of how you connect to yourself? So I tend to wring my hands, rub my face and give myself mini pep talks when faced with some challenge (say in the gym when tired but I have not completed a planned workout). So take a moment and write down how you connect to yourself, again this awareness will help you as you go about connecting to others:

_____

_____

_____

_____.

A third idea that you might find useful is a discussion about what comes out of your mouth to promote change. This would be the area where you would expect each of the schools to offer different ideas about how to make change and that is the case. For me I use the structural ideas we discussed in terms of tracking conversations, and I try to always be self-aware but the types of questions I ask tend to come from the post-modern schools such as the collaborative therapy of Bill Madsen (2007)- which are heavy influenced by narrative therapy or solution-focused work of Insoo Kim Berg (1994). In plain English, this means I try to ask a lot of curious questions. When an externalization comes along as we discussed in chapter twelve, I run with it. I always look for exceptions (this is especially helpful with you who often talk using "always/never" type proclamations) or explore how folks coped with adversity. When I want to activate internal motivation, scaling questions are useful.

So the three preceding paragraphs hopefully I have laid out an integrative way of working that is very much informed by practice theory while allowing us to use various models into a holistic approach. I want to stress that this is just a way I come to think about family work. It is by no means the right way, whatever that is. I do think that exploring what each of the schools of thought have to have makes sense. I do think that if you know where you got something from will help you feel more confident and if you get the opportunity to dive into a school and practice it exclusively, that is excellent experience, even if you do not exclusively use it for the rest of your professional career, the knowledge alone will make it worth it.

Berg, I.K. (1994). *Family Based Services: A Solution-Focused Approach.* NY, NY: Norton.

Madesn, W. (2007). *Collaborative Therapy with Multi-Stressed Families.* NY, NY: Guilford.

Minuchin, S. & Fishman, H.C. (1981). *Family Therapy Techniques.* Cambridge, MA: Harvard University Press.

Satir, V. (1967). *Conjoint Family Therapy.* Palo Alto, CA: Science & Behavior Books.

White, M. & Epson, D. (1990). *Narrative Means to Therapeutic Ends.* NY, NY: Norton.

Family practice: Getting deeper into the work

Ok let us say that you have engaged with the families that you are working with and that you have been invited into their home and that you have some understanding of what the issues are. Yet now there seems to be a fly in the ointment. One area that many practitioners I know will report is doing family work is that they can feel like the train is off the tracks, that they lose direction (on purpose there are no drawings here of all those juicy metaphors as we do not want to put too much stock in what is not going well). Often times, it may seem that there are too many agendas, too much going on, competing demands to make the kind of progress that all made a commitment to do in the first place. As much as possible in these moments when it seems like things are not going well, to pay attention to the process. Even if that involves resisting the temptation of getting more complicated and trying some super intervention, try to keep it simple. Reflect on the idea that "how we are going is as important as how we get there"- I do not have a citation for that. This all comes from the keep it simple school. One way to do this is to slow folks down and say "let's see if we can get on the same page". I often will give a mini speech about how it seems today that everyone is in their own camps and in doing so ignores the commonality that they have. So I will start by saying "let's start with *Respect, how does this family show respect to one another*?" If an argument arises, push them to say when respect is happening as opposed to when it is not happening. See if you can work to a shared agreement on the value of respect and how that value is something that defines their family. Respect may seem like a general topic but it is actually a core issue that pretty much every family I have ever met holds as important and is willing to talk about. Promoting a discussion of how this particular family can rally around the flag of respect will help you get everyone on the same page and that will help you regain momentum and quiet the voices that "this isn't working".

Following the respect conversation, you can repeat the process with the concept of *Trust*. Trust, may not have as much street value as respect but it is not far behind. This is especially powerful in families with youth or preteens where trust questions are just part of the developmental process. Again your job is intercept blaming communications and instead work with the family to get them to explain what trust looks like, what the parameters of trust are, the expectations for every member regarding trust and to hear full examples of when trust was being shown. This is story work, I know I am partial to stories, the thinking here is that the telling of the positive story helps to shape the reality that they are a family in which they value trustful and respectful relationships. Working in this way you block two real porcupines of family work:

The two porcupines are feeling like we are not a whole and allowing we/they thinking to operate inside a family. While these may be simple ideas, experience has shown time and again how the two porcupines can really stick it to a family. Our society, with the high rates of divorce, media attention to gender differences and a slew of reality shows that demonstrate to us all that we are not on the same page, tend to feed the porcupines. Your job is to be on guard for them and if and when they appear, to gently stop the process and pull for some sense of the whole

As a general rule, when working with a family I am trying to activate their skills as a system to have the kind of interactions, conversations and make the type of decisions for their family that they would prefer. While I know most families do not sit around and plan out how they want their family to be, but they do, in general know. By using a series of curious questions, you can activate that type of conversation. Once people have said something out loud, they will be more motivated to do it. A simple and long standing family technique is called "circular questioning". Circular questioning is when you ask a question to a family member about another or other family members in front of them. The value of it is that it helps the family and its members gain perspective that only another member can really give them. There are a number of very natural content areas that you can use circular questioning in. For instance, you can ask about relationships: To a father you might say, "Throughout time mothers and daughters are famous for their relationships, how do your wife and your daughter get along?" From there encourage stories that define and illuminate the story. This will flesh out the multiple dimensions of the relationship that may have become flattened by the weight of the challenges. A personal favorite of mine is to ask about family routine. I often will draw a clock:

With the clock you can ask about all types of family process.

Such as "a lot of families with kids will tell me that the hour or two between getting everyone out of bed and onto the school bus is like running a three ring circus, walk me through a typical morning in your house, who does what, what is the good, bad and ugly of that part of the day?" Here the questioning works to normalize and generalize but also illuminate all the positive coping that is going on but is being missed by virtue of the routine (and perhaps the sleep deprivation). A third type of circular questioning is a rift on a solution-focused scaling question, basically asking a ranking question: "If you have some really good news, who is the first person you want to tell in the family and how come?" Or, "if you have to have a punishment, who would you least like to get it from?" While that second question is tricky, I encourage you to model open dialogue. In truth punishment or consequences happen in every family, so to me it is fair and actually important stuff to talk about. Every once in a while, what comes out is something that, as a mandated reporter I have to deal with, if it does I deal with it. As an aside, I will tell people I have to report that but also counsel them on the role that protective services plays and that no one is out to "steal their babies" – that just is not the job of the hard working and much maligned people at child protective services. Time is a great topic for circular questioning. Many therapeutic approaches have written about time, perhaps the narrative therapists most successfully. In any event, "how was life different when you lived on Darwin street?" Simple question but it opens up a potential flood of dialogue between the members. Remember it is not the content we are always going for but trying to activate family process. There can be tons of others, but one last one that I see as critical is what I call the "missing member formation" – named after a air force jet flying formation- crudely drawn here to honor someone who is not there.

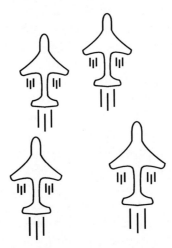

Recall that we started the whole family section with the idea that everyone has a family, even if it is just a whisper or a faint memory, to that end it is important to ask about folks who are not present for one reason or another: "if dad were hear, listening to you talk, what do you think he would say about all this?" I had the great privilege to tape a session with Bill Madsen as he talked with a youth about her deceased mother in a way that brought the mother into the room, overcoming the sadness for the kid and replacing it, at least for a moment with a different emotion, as she talked about how she was sure her mom would be proud of the woman she was becoming. This can also be used with a member who is silent. For instance, "we know that Jane prefers not to say much in these family meetings, but she is always here and always listening, what do you think she is thinking?" Incidentally this often will provoke the quieter member to correct the misperception. In sum, work to activate family process without regard for an agenda, the family has the capacity to address its own challenges; our role is to just get them going.

Externalization with Families

In chapter twelve we discussed externalization and explained it, I want to go back to it again and go a little deeper and apply it to family work. Recall I mentioned that in explaining the concept I often pull an empty chair forward and explain that that is where the challenge/problem is. Here is a drawing of an empty chair to remind you of the idea.

One of the challenges in family work that has been long identified is that often in families there is an identified "scapegoat" this is the family ner-do-well who always seems to mess up or mess things up. As the story life of the family progresses the mess ups become increasingly predictable so that when things bad go down this person is blamed, even if there was no way they could have been involved. As we have discussed, one of the great contributions of family therapy is that problems or challenges are defined interactively as opposed to being placed at the feet of any one person. So in general most family minded social work practitioners hear the challenge as an interactive one. If you can do this you are well on your way to being able to externalize the challenge so that it lives outside of any one family member but is something that all members do have to interact with. It is important to say that the point is not to excuse personal responsibility, but rather to create some space to the challenge can be worked on. Let us turn to the perfect example of an issue that is often seen as an individual issue but can benefit from externalization; alcoholism. Alcoholism is terrible, difficult to beat, destructive and prevalent. Alcoholism is tough on families. No doubt you know there is some biological evidence of transmission across generations in families. The largest single way alcoholism is treated is through a 12 step program which involves the person admitting to their alcoholism. Given the general success of this approach, it is hard to criticize it, but hopefully all would agree that it is not particularly strength based, at least at first. Externalization does offer another path to recovery. Here is how it would look: The Smith family consists of Dad- Bob, Mother- Alice, Sisters Carol and Jennifer. Bob has a long history of alcohol abuse, despite periods of sobriety, currently he is drinking. Recently he was terminated from his employment due to an alcohol related work performance issue. Alice has informed him that she thinks that it is best if she takes the girls to live with her mother as a separation. Bob begs her to and the girls to come with him to see the latest clinical social worker he has just started to work with, Alice agrees noting her patience is "just about gone". The new social worker follows a Bill Madsen type collaborative interview. Collaborative therapy is basically a first cousin to narrative therapy, much of the differences are academic, but with regard to externalization there is an important distinction. Where narrative therapy uses externalization as an intervention, a collaborative therapist would see externalization as an on-going core of the work. So Bob is seen as a man who is engaged in a intense relationship with alcohol. So much so that the relationship with alcohol clouds over his family and many other aspects of his life. Here is Bob and his family under the Bottle Clouds which are blocking most but not all of the light.

The social worker would always start by getting to know the family outside of the influence of the challenge. As an aside, no matter what you do, consider getting to know people as people first, often times, people come to first meetings bursting to discuss all that is wrong, I found it works a lot better for me to know them as people and it tends to relax people to talk about things other than the weight of the challenges. With an engaging conversation hopefully you can move forward to a conversation about the challenge that is facing the family. With the family in this example they all (Bob included) say the challenge is Bob's alcoholism. They have a lot of stories of ruined sleep overs, dinner parties, vacations, jobs and so forth. At this point the externalization has often appeared, here we move from the problem of Bob the alcoholic to Bob's relationship with alcohol and the effect that alcohol has over everyone in the family. With alcohol now sitting in a chair in the room, the social worker can explore the contexts that alcohol operates best and also the context when alcohol is least effective or not present. This also opens the door to ask the family about the larger social-cultural world that alcohol works in. Here in America, the fact is that alcohol never sleeps. There is a 24/7/365 ad content telling us that friends, get-togethers, good times, sports, the beach, romance and so forth all go better with alcohol. Yes we should drink responsibly but we should drink. Bob is under constant pressure to "have a couple beers". As the conversation moves forward, you can use the externalization with the family to expand the circle. You can ask about history with the challenge. In that history you can ask about times when things were better and when they were worse and what was happening at those times. You can ask what other supports alcohol has on its side and what other supports the forces the family has on its side and how to mobilize them. Working this way you hear about what Madsen would say are the things that constrain the family from being the way they prefer to be and have an honest discussion about the way they would prefer to be. In general the idea is that it is good for the family to talk about how they would like to be a family. In fact the idea is that it is better for them to talk about how they desire to be, then it is to talk about splitting up unless that is what they want.

Working in this way the whole family uses the externalization to move past blame and to become motivated and unified in the fight against the oppressive force that has occupied perhaps the biggest chair in the family. The beauty of the approach is that you do very much talk about the challenge that is present; there is no "rose-colored hippy-dippy glasses" because you are into the issue, but it is presented really as a constraining force. The externalization turns the adjective into a noun, a noun that is in relationship with the family. This pulls forward motivation and creates energy and space for change which is opposite from the way that blame tends to deflate motivation and energy. It is important for us to think about how change actually happens. Perhaps, think about a change that you (the reader) have made and sustained. What motivated you? What sustained you? While I am sure that shame and blame do work sometimes as a motivator for change, but if we really are involved in being useful to people in making sustained change in their lives, than let us get behind the movement towards something exciting, verses trying to avoid a negative, as that invites hopelessness and frustration to the dance.

On Group Practice

If you are a history buff then you know that social work practice started out largely as group practice. Social workers have always run groups; it is a practice specialty of the profession. There is a lot to talk about when considering group practice. Of course there are tons of books on the subject. Consistent with the approach of this book, I always will recommend a seminal text in any area as a start. In the case of group work, the bible, if you will, was written by Yalom. Great book - doubles nicely if you have a small child and forgot the booster seat, as it is thick. The cool thing about group practice is that pretty much all of us get taught group in a class that is run as a group, which is to say that reading about group work is not anywhere near as effective as being in a group. After graduate school, I had the good fortune of being trained by one of my mentors (Dr. F.) in group work by completing a Bion style group experience, which has served me well forever. While I do not practice in a Bion or Tavistock manner as it is more widely known as, the training helped me to understand the dynamics of group work on a deep level. So while people do not always like classes in which one is graded on their group work, the process you went through is invaluable. So let us walk through some core ideas about group work. For the purpose of being focused, this chapter is about therapeutic groups. There are other chapters about teamwork that will address ideas about task groups.

Hopefully we can all agree on the value of therapeutic group work, which is generally described as some form of mutual aid. The most often cited value of group is members helping members through accessing the universality of experience. If isolation, shame and loss are at the root of so many of the challenges that people face, group is an ideal place to provide a therapeutic experience to address these challenging issues. Perhaps a story or two will back up and illuminate the point. For a great number of years I had the distinct honor of running a group for grandmothers who were raising their grandchildren through the kinship foster care system after the parent (s) of the child had become unable to do so largely due to crack cocaine. The group was held in midtown Manhattan and the grandmothers would take trains and buses from Queens, Brooklyn and the Bronx to come for the weekly group. Along the way they labeled themselves "the ducks". I incorrectly assumed (always a bad move to assume) that the name came from how they would always brave the cold rain and snow to get to group. While they acknowledged that more often than they would like they did have to battle the elements to get to group, they told me the name had a deeper meaning. The group members were proud women, most had been born in the rural South and moved to New York as part of the great migration of African American families after the second world war. They felt guilty and responsible that their own child (often a daughter) had become addicted to crack. Although they did not know why their own child had turned to drugs, it evoked shame and ate away at their pride. They explained that they were ducks because if you see a duck on a pond they appear to be gliding across the pond effortlessly. This is the way they wished the world to see them, gliding effortlessly across the pond of life. In reality they were like ducks though because under the waterline their feet like that of real life ducks, were constantly scrambling to keep up, to raise this next generation "right"- many of which were now teenagers who presented a host of challenges- and group, they said, was the one place they could talk about that struggle without feeling judged. The women bonded together and talked, told stories and supported one another in a way that made being with this group my favorite time of the work week. Here are my ducks:

Story # 2, right after I finished my group training, I was assigned to co-lead a group that no one wanted to work with. The agency offered a group for mothers who had lost their parental rights due to mental illness. Terminating parental rights solely on the grounds of mental illness is rare- abandonment, permanent neglect or abuse is much more common. These women loved their children; they came to visit them while they were in foster care, they complied with court orders to jump through this hoop or that one, but in the end of the day the court had found that their mental health challenges were such that they needed to lose their rights to their children forever. Although the agency as an organization, wanted the group, most of the staff did not as the women were often loud, disruptive and would steal the toilet paper. The women, among other things were very angry at their situation and the self-appointed leader of the group was downright vicious in the verbal attacks she could dish out. I often felt like I was in a circus, specifically in the lion cage, no whip, no chair, just waiting to be eaten alive. The thing of it was, they had each other's back. Their own sense of isolation, fear and not knowing what value they had since they could not be moms to their kids bound them together tightly. So while it was not a fun group to run, the value of the mutual aid was an amazing thing to see. The lesson here is that when we work to gain mutual aid, in many ways it is the most deeply therapeutic thing we can do.

The question then is, how do we start a group so we get that type of mutual aid thing going? Starting a group is labor intensive. Since there are so many types of groups (psychoeducation, play therapy, socialization, dialectical behavioral to name a few) it is important to be clear what you want to do. This involves the question of structure. You need to know what your intent is. You need to know if the group will be a closed group so that membership does not change or it is open so people can come and go. You need to decide if the group will be time limed (for instance 12 weeks) or on-going. Therapeutic groups tend to run 60 to 90 minutes, but a socialization group for fifth grade boys maybe runs 30 minutes. In a similar way you need to talk about frequency, with weekly being most common but there are plenty of reasons to meet less or more often. You have to decide if you are going to use a curriculum and if you do, you need to go over it closely. I have watched any number of folks download some anger management stuff off the web and try to run a group only to have it be rejected by the members as they found the activities insulting. It is important to consider the membership. How are you going to get members? Are you going to screen them? How wide can you go with the challenges the members present. Generally in my experience, the more the challenges are homogeneous, the better chance we had at getting the mutual aid thing going. You need to think about food, will you have food? Is there a budget for food? Would the members be in a position to rotate and bring food, or would that be a set up for disaster? Is the space where you are going to have the group contusive to a group? We could probably have a whole chapter on the pros and cons of a table or not. Obviously if you are running an activity group with a craft as is often done in children's socialization groups, you need a table. By and large people like tables as they feel more grounded and safe but if you watch the old master tapes on group work, they rarely had tables. For what it is worth the ducks had a table the moms who had lost their children via termination did not. Finally how many leaders will you have? If you have more than just yourself, then I strongly suggest that the leaders spend time together discussing style, expectations and practice beliefs before ever starting to form the group, as you do need to be on the same page structurally (we will talk about leadership more in a moment).

So you got all the stuff in the preceding paragraph attended to, now you are in the room for the very first time, how do you get group process going? For me knowing where the group is at as a group has always informed me on what the group needs from me and how active I should be. That said I have always been a fan of Bruce Tuckman's *Orming* model. There are other stage models and there are critiques of this model. What I have found is if you think about the model in a non-rigid way- so that maybe there is no storming, or you may move between stages in a non-linear way- that is fine. The beauty of the model in my mind is to get a sense of the group and what they need from the leader. A new group is forming. That means they need the leader to be active. In a new group, people are unsure if the group will be good for them, the more I can help make people feel comfortable, welcomed and safe, the better. Ice breaker type games/activities will work well. An early goal is the members learning each other's names. To support this, one group activity that you can lead is to make group "rules" this would be a loose use of the word, the objective is less to have a rule and more to create some shared buy-in about how we wish to be with each other. So the tone of the conversation that you have as well as your ability to attend to process of the group is essential in any rules discussion. Not all groups go into storming, and not all groups that do storm do so as a marked stage after forming. However if you have been in a group that got into a storming phase, you most likely remember it. Here is a dark cloud dropping some heavy rain down:

Storming is about sense of safety including a sense of if the leader (s) can handle the group. This means you need to be active, more active than in any other time. As much as possible try to avoid the content of the challenges that are being expressed and stick to the process of what is going on. Help people feel safe and model that you are ok being with the group. Demonstrate that you can handle the group. One particular group with the mothers who had their rights terminated always sticks out as the prime number one example of the leadership challenge of a group that is storming. I have no memory of how it all got started but I recall the self-appointed leader, in an indignant rage, face red, words coming out a mile a minute accusing me of wanting to do all manner of sexual acts with her. My first reaction was "no that is not the case" but that only fueled the fire and escalated the attacks, it was vile to put it nicely. By switching to the process I was able to attend to the dynamic of the storming. I made comments about "we all have the challenge of being in group where you don't know people that well, which make can make anyone feel vulnerable". This connected with the underlying fear and that brought the affect down. If I had the skill as an artist I would draw the knuckles on my hand turned white from gripping the chair arm so hard, it was terrifying, but the group needed me to stay calm and not freak out and not run away. The group did not see my knuckles, what they saw was that I hung in there (I wanted to run believe me) and that made them safe.

As mentioned, the leadership demands of the forming and storming stages are high. Groups, in my mind are best served by having co-leaders that can sit across from each. What co-leadership does is allow one leader to be active and the other leader to observe and then flip roles, so at least one leader can "see" the whole group process at one time. To achieve this level of leadership, you and your co-leader need to talk before and after every group to process out your plan. Sitting across from each other allows for non-verbal communication between you two. Pretty much every group I have ever run had co-leaders, except due to agency turnover I had gone through four co-leaders with the grandmother group and the grandmothers themselves asked to not have the disruption of "another young thing that will leave in six months".

In general what group work strives to do is to work in the present, to stay in the room, even if the conversation moves outside of the room, keeping the focus in the room activates the group process. For example, the kinship grandmothers did talk a lot about the woes of their daughters, but we worked to use the group members to loop back around to how they themselves are handling the various challenges and disappointments. This is often best done by what I call the *lob shot*. I borrow this from tennis. If you watch a professional tennis match, much of the action is about smashing the ball back and forth, but often points can be won my simply lobbing a shot into the middle of a court. In group practice you can gently lob to the middle. This is a comment that is not directed at any one member but the group as a whole. For instance "right now we are talking about the shame and disappointment of having a daughter that seems to prefer the crack pipe over her own kids". The purpose is to activate the group process without putting anyone on the spot. The lob shot pulls for the universality of experience while allowing you as the leader to say something that might be hard for anyone to say and frankly it is so much more useful than the typical "can anyone else relate?" Here is the lob shot:

Staying focused on the process and content in tandem helps to stay in the present. Early on I co-lead a group in an adult acute psychiatric hospital for people with schizophrenia, I doubt that I was able to keep that group focused but the members seemed to enjoy the time, even if I struggled to facilitate a sense of group.

The successful group achieves a norming stage and the rare group achieves a performing stage where the members report how much they "love group" and work hard with each other. The more advanced in the process a group goes, the less the leader needs to do. Tuckman would add a *transforming* stage related to termination work. As with all termination work, this is an active time for us. We should help folks to solidify the gains they have made and gain perspective of the hard work that they have done that has led to change in their lives. For time limited groups, adding a planned transforming including some celebration of the work makes sense to me, people should have a sense of accomplishment when they do something challenging.

Tuckman, B. W., & Jensen, M. A. C. (1977). Stages of small-group development revisited. *Group & Organization Management, 2*(4), 419-427.

Yalom, I. D., & Leszcz, M. (2005). *Theory and practice of group psychotherapy*. Basic books.

Setting the stage for macro practice: The river of lost souls

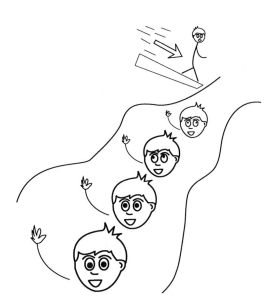

Above is one of the first drawings I ever used in class. I use it to illustrate the point of intervention when doing macro work. I came to the drawing honestly through my work with children and families in the child welfare, children's mental health and children infected/affected by HIV/AIDS systems. Slowly it dawned on me that I was working with the same case over and over. Sure the names and faces changed but the stories were all too similar. Like a light in the distance that gets brighter and brighter as you get closer to it, I began to realize that no matter how skilled I got being useful to people in helping them get out of what we can call the "river of lost souls", there were too many people in that river and perhaps I should start investigating who or what was pushing them into the river and see if I could do something about that. This chapter and the chapters that follow related to macro practice have a strong underpinning to social, economic and environmental justice. I mention that not as a warning but rather to make sure you know the foundation upon which macro practice springs from. The questions we can ask could be things like "why do we build homeless shelters instead of solving homelessness?" or "why are there food pantries instead of solving hunger?" Clearly we have enough housing and enough food for every living person in this country. Are homelessness and hunger too big for us to tackle successfully? Actually they are solvable challenges, we just get conned into believing that it is too hard, too complex, or too political to do so. This chapter and the chapters following it are about the beauty and necessity of macro practice.

As we are talking about a much larger playing field it is critical that we have a holistic mindset to use to make sense of the complex challenges that we are talking about in macro work. Things such as[racism, sexism, classism, poverty, homelessness, AIDS, Veteran suicide, suicide in general, homicide, substance abuse, neighborhood decay] and so forth. In the late 1980's Ruth Parsons coined "integrated practice" as a way to holistically think about social challenges. What was brilliant was the shift from thinking that our job was to rehabilitate people- to pull them from the river and rather our efforts, in a very holistic manner and using a collection of roles and skills, is to target the issue.

The issues are complex. There is a non-sumativity to the issues- that $1 + 1$ does not equal 2 but rather 3 or 4. I like to explain this idea by thinking of the great American 1960 rock group, the Mommas and the Poppas (they wrote a string of hits including *California Dreaming*). See the group consisted of two Mommas- Momma Cass and Michelle Phillips and two Poppas- John Phillips and Denny Doherty. What they attributed their success to was that when their four voices combined a fifth voice emerged out of the blend. In the same way poverty interacts with racism and neighborhood decay to produce a more complex challenge than any one of the three alone does. The integrated perspective is built upon the three legged stool of **systems thinking** (we talked about this at length in the family therapy chapters), **strength-based thinking** (we thank Dennis Saleebey for this excellent contribution) and **empowerment.** For those of you who have not gone old school and read Barbara Solomon and her thoughts on empowerment in America, do yourself a favor, the citation is at the bottom of this chapter. Ok stop reading for a moment and ask yourself this question "How would I go about increasing the level of pride in the community I live in?"

What did you come up with? Not so simple right? But in your ideas were there systems concepts? Did you build upon existing community assets? Did you think about actualizing the power of your neighbors? We will build on these themes, because this work is essential to your macro practice skill set and in truth to our society.

Parsons, R., Jorgensen, J. & Hernandez, S. (1988). Integrated practice: A framework for Problem solving. *Social Work*. Oct.-Nov. 417-421.

Saleebey, D. (1992). *The Strengths Perspective in Social Work Practice*. Boston: Pearson.

Solomon, B. (1976). *Black Empowerment: Social Work in Oppressed Communities*. NY: Columbia University Press.

"Without justice there can be no love"

24
Chapter

The title of this chapter is taken from a bell hooks quote. When we are being honest about community practice we need to acknowledge the tensions that exist in our society. America was started as a democracy to escape the perceived tyranny of a ruling class. While democracy does not mean that everyone should have the same, should there not be real social justice where everyone has access to the same resources? I hope that we can agree that we have challenges in our society. The challenges seem most notable in sectors in our society. The urban centers of many cities and many of the rural spaces on America are sectors they seem to carry an unequal amount of the burden of social, economic, environmental injustice.

This is a practice text, we can leave it to others for an in-depth study of the how-comes. I ask that you hold (lightly) the premise that the injustice has been socially constructed via a number of factors so that we can focus on what to do about it.

In response to the challenges there are two general approaches to make change. The traditional approach, which is the one that is most often employed, is begun by some kind of needs assessment related to the problems and then building programs to address those problems (as a reader you may have noticed that the "P" word is not used in this text, "challenges" is the term used here, as challenge implies the ability to overcome, the word problem is only used here as purposeful then as it is reflected of the traditional mindset). As well intentioned and used as the traditional path is, it does activate what Barbara Solomon calls "negative valuation". This is the idea that the negative forces surrounding a person tend to get internalized to the extent that the person buys into them and acts as if there are a truth. Thereby a potentially unwanted byproduct of the traditional path of addressing macro level challenges is that the people most affected by the issue are cut out and all the energy, attention and money are directed at a service. The service then is in the positon of fixing the problem. This then reinforces disempowerment, as the people have been relegated to being consumers of services. Their own expertise is not asked for and they do not control the purse strings.

For some time, John McKnight among others has been championing an asset-based approach to address the challenges in a community. The idea is fairly simple, to make a map of all the local assets in a community and then begin connecting in such a way that their asset comes forth. Strengths are often buried or ignored as the focus is on what is not working. Part of the brilliance of McKnight's approach is the simple truth that every single community is asset rich. Our job is to help that truth become apparent or re-apparent. It is important to note that communities can be place based such as the Avenue D neighborhood or they can be communities of affiliation such as the community of children of deployed soldiers. For place based communities, start with the gifts of the individuals with special attention to individuals that are often overlooked such as the elderly, youth, people of color, people with disabilities. Next look to the gifts in associational life. Now some associations are formal such as the local Rotary club and some are informal, such as the group of women who formed a book club in the Long Meadows neighborhood or the group of folks that own a snow blower together to clear the driveways and walks in winter months. As a practitioner, your job is to locate the associational life in a community as it is a rich source of assets as the people are already getting together. Finally locate the formal institutions in the community- these are the brick and motor places that also are rich in assets. Schools are a great source for assets. In addition to the job of educating the children, they provide space for all kinds of community groups. One day I went to pick up one of my daughters from softball practice and discovered a group of older women practice the Japanese sword fighting martial art known as Kendo in the gym. If you look at the community like a set of Russian nesting or stacking Matryoshka dolls, you are well on your way to seeing the assets in a holistic manner.

Now let us circle back around to the bell hooks quote that started this chapter. Your assessment is just a start, the real work is using your relational skills to get people to mobilize, to want to work together. The work is to use your networking skills to catalyze a reaction where the community starts to take charge to make it better, to bring about justice. This is the heart of community development work: To attack the injustice. Maybe it is the task of getting a playground built as there is no safe space for kids to play or maybe it is forming a neighborhood watch. Your job is to seed the ground and then watch for the organic growth and the organic leaders that emerge. This is bottom-up social justice work

McKnight, J. & Block, J. (2010). *The Abundant Community: Awakening the Power of Families and Neighborhoods*. S.F.: Berret-Koehler.

Community practice AKA "Staying in the Mess"

While there remains important work to be done, one of the most successful and longest standing social justice movements has been the women's rights movement. A fantastic bi-product of the women's rights movement has been the development of feminist thought and writings. Feminism addresses many things but in application to social justice work, the holistic and empowerment –based approach does provide a real pathway to successful practice. From a feminist perspective, empowerment has been transformed away from a rather modest endeavor aimed at adapting or coping to a process of actualizing power. This has been vital, especially in oppressed communities. Oppression is not an abstract topic, for too many in this country, it is an everyday reality. It is a major force that is pushing people into that river we talked about a couple chapters back. Oppression breeds apathy, hopelessness and disconnection. Empowerment promotes the idea that a person can have a voice, a person can make change, that things don't just have to stay the same. As community-minded practitioners we have a role in promoting empowerment. The first thing we have to do is go get into the mess. That means we have to join the people where they are at. As nice as our offices may or may not be, we need to get into the community. Similar to the value of a home visit to family practice, community practice needs to be done in the community. This is where those community institutions come in handy. Schools, churches, fast food restaurants are meeting spaces for people to gather, to connect and to plan for change. We are talking about social justice that means we are talking about power. Directly the message here, is to give up the power that comes with your office and get out to the community. As the title, which comes from a community building article by Salmon & Steinberg, suggests sometimes it is messy out there. We had been invited to do some community building work in a small neighborhood beset by violence, poverty and hopelessness. We did some door to door activism to work to promote neighbor to neighbor group on a day in March with a long winter's snowfall moldering to reveal months of trash, alcohol bottles and used syringes-the students found it messy, but to my delight persisted through the mess to see the beauty of people coming together to reclaim their neighborhood. In truth the mess is more than trash revealed by melting snow, the mess we are talking about is what happens when you are doing community building from the bottom up. As example is when you are working to have communities define themselves and what they want to work on (rather than telling them what to work on). This is slow and perhaps challenging to start but once it gains traction then the community will run with it and sustain it and ultimately that is what it is all about, in the meantime, We (practitioners) need to gain comfort being in the mess of the community building process,

You know what else is messy? Democracy is messy. What we have today in America seems to be a bit of confusion. It would appear that some folks are confusing rampant capitalism with democracy. These are two different ideas. This is not a critique of capitalism but clearly as the gap in America between the "haves" and the "have-nots" widens, there are folks on the bottom who feel pushed aside of the system. Community building aims to re-engage them. So I am planting the flag right here in honor of the good old democratic work that is community building.

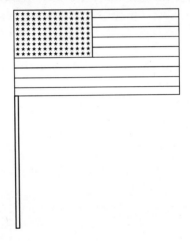

As we approach this work, if we are clear on our role as change agents who can facilitate or catalyze community building activity then we have positioned ourselves correctly. We may be the best positioned to see strengths in a community, to see the ways that a diversity of voice makes efforts stronger and able to elicit diverse representation at the community building table. As we support a sense of participatory democratic action, then the community can gain and realize its own power and make the change it wants. It is about bringing gifts forwards. Just so we are not asking others to do what we cannot do, take a moment and write below what is a gift (or two) that you bring to community building work. Remember when you write something down it grows

Salmon, R. and Steinberg, D. M. 2007. Staying in the mess: Teaching students and practitioners to work effectively in the swamp of important problems. *Social Work with Groups*, 30 4, 79–94.

Jack Rothman's three legged stool

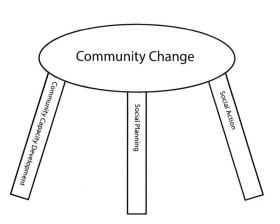

That is a drawing of me throwing a stone. It is a warning about the intent behind this final macro chapter and a reminder of the work that is to be done. For social work programs to grant licensable degrees they need to be accredited. The accreditation work is done by the Council on Social Work Education (CSWE). CSWE holds a huge and excellent conference every year. Here comes the stone: It is a real shame that more folks go to sessions about the CSWE rules than they go to sessions on making community change, year after year I see this. It really bothers me that more social work educators are drawn for whatever reason- and there are good reasons to go to sessions on learning on how to dot the "I" and cross the "t" instead of how to roll up the shirt sleeve and get it done in the mess. One advantage of not having a ton of people in the community practice sessions is that it has allowed me to get to talk to one of the professions true giants, Jack Rothman, who has outlined how to do community work, first as a three legged stool of *locality development, social action and social planning* (he later changed locality development to *community capacity development* to acknowledge that not all communities are place based) and later as a more matrix like nine part design. To me the simple three legged idea is just perfect and I encourage one and all to read up on it. That said I will do the briefest of summary to whet your appetite, again the real thing is better:

Community capacity development is the most democratic form of making community change. The entire purpose to get people involved. It is the quintessential grassroots operation. While change is always an end goal, the process used here is paramount, as the effort must be made to mobile the people to be involved and actually to work alongside of the power sources to bring about change. In the community I live in, we have started a not-for-profit to end murder. It is a work in progress but every community forum that is followed by a free spaghetti dinner cooked by the hospitality committee of some local church is a victory. Every time we go door to door and talk with neighbors about their community, we have achieved part of our goal to activate the power of the community to address a challenge it faces. Relationships are assets, use them to make change. To be clear, murder is a behavior and behaviors can be changed, we can create community without murder.

Social planning probably gets a bad name because it seems rather dry and data driven, but in fact we have had great success in mobilizing people to work with the power sources to make changes in the physical environments in which we live. Elected officials actually generally enjoy being able to point to improvements made while they were in charge. So the dog parks, speed bumps installed on streets where the drivers were endangering children, and the community gardens that have been built are not dry, they are powerful reminders that we can have a say in how our public spaces are developed.

Social action is in many ways the best known type of community change activity. Social action follows from the premise that sometimes there are forces that will not move so you have to move them (that reminds me, when doing community work it is always a good idea to do a *force field analysis*- see the Brage and Holloway citation below). Social action is when we use pressure to make things move. A personal favorite comes from the late 1960's when Saul Alinsk was brought to Rochester, NY to try to help convince Eastman Kodak (the camera and film company) to integrate their workforce. Kodak would not budge so he organized a *fart-in* (I will let your imagination draw that one) at the local symphony which was a Kodak gem. The news it generated brought Kodak to the table.

To sum these last few chapters up, a healthy community is a form of living democracy. It is a place where people are working together to address the things that matter to them. The biggest room in the house, is the room for improvement. As members of our respective communities, we have a duty to shape the basic conditions that affect our lives. Gathering folks together to work for common purpose is the root of our profession and remains a vital practice activity.

Brager, G., & Holloway, S. (1993). Assessing prospects for organizational change: The uses of force field analysis. *Administration in Social Work, 16,* 3-4, 15-28.

Rothman, J. (1970). Three models of community organization practice. *Strategies of Community Organization: Macro Practice. Itasca, IL: Peacock Publishers Inc,* 20-35.

The value of being a good team member

In many ways this chapter harkens back to some of the discussion from the group chapter. The quick and dirty of the chapter goes like this: Most of us will spend the majority of our professional lives working in an organization of some kind (social service, chemical dependency, hospital, school ect.). In those organizations we will be asked to work on and with teams of people. Some of those teams will be on-going, others will be shorter term work teams, but they all are groups and they operate as groups do. Here is the kicker:

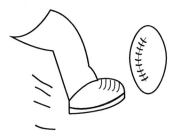

Your success in the working with the teams you are assigned to (as mostly you do not get to choose the team you work with) is to apply group understanding to your teamwork to make the team's functioning and your enjoyment of the teamwork the best it can possibly be. So we are back to a process and content discussion. There is the *what* of teamwork and there is the *how* of teamwork, paying attention to both is the golden road to success.

A good while back some unknown person noticed that in the animal kingdom there is a bird that has figured out teamwork, that is the goose (if you go on line, you will see folks claiming this idea as theirs but truth is it has been around way longer than the internet). Geese are interesting creatures. Given their large size and weight, they would not be an ideal choice to be a long flyer, but they are in fact migratory birds that fly long distances to their different seasonal habitats.

The secret to their success is believed to be the V formation and the process they use to maintain the V. Scientists will tell you that by flying in a V the birds trailing after the leader get a lift which allows them to use less energy. A similar sized bird, the pelican, which does not usually use the V has been found to have much higher heart rates when flying as they are doing all the work, consequently pelicans don't tend to fly that far. The way the V works is that a goose will lead for a while, then rotate to the back and another takes over. We will talk about leadership in the next chapter, but it is important to note that they do rotate leadership to keep it fresh at the top. The V also has the advantage of knowing where everyone is, as it is harder to lose someone, as no one just goes off on their own.

Applying the geese metaphor to teams leads us to a couple important points: First is that for teams to be effective there has to be agreement about where they are going. I imagine that most of us can think of a time when we were working on a team that lacked direction or worked at cross purpose. This is a truly frustrating experience to have and sadly it is not uncommon. On the surface this does not make sense, as teams are organized around a common purpose, in practice it just is not that simple. Anyone that has even a passing interest in sports has seen teams trying to ensure a championship by loading up on all the best players only to watch that manufactured team not be able to produce and collapse into a pile of finger pointing. Again the objective was clear: win, the process is where it broke down. The geese keep it simple; they use a winning and proven process. The old adage, "there is no 'I' in team" or "no one can whistle a symphony, you need an orchestra to play it" all speak to the need to create interdependency. To me, social workers are born team leaders. I know I am biased because my practice has largely been in social service agencies where social workers are thrust into that role, but regardless of type or place of employment, the skills that social workers are trained with make us excellent team members and by extension team leaders. As a leader you can be useful to your team by helping to make sure that everyone is on the same page. You can do process checks. That is simply by raising your hand and asking how do people see us working together right now? Or you can use some type of time marker on the life of the team to ask if we are meeting the goals we set out for ourselves. You can help a team write a mission statement for the team and keep it as a living document. All these activities help the V fly and work to ensure that no one gets lost.

Behind the approach of keeping the V in good flying shape is you bringing your assessment skills to the team. Start with yourself. What role are you playing on the team? If you are on multiple teams, do you always play a similar role or do the dynamics of the team require you to take on different roles in different teams? Ask yourself what are the behaviors that you are doing that is supporting your role and the work of the team? This is not navel gazing, it is the essence of self-directed practice to be aware of what you are doing. Being able to verbalize what your specific contributions to the team are will help you feel more effective in the murky waters of team work. Now what are the other roles that you see in operation on the team? You can use a Johari window as a team exercise to bring forward greater understanding of the roles on a team. In many ways a team in which there is some flexibility in roles is in best position to be successful. I learned this lesson some years back on a 23 day outward bound experience. Our team had unofficially let one person do the lion's share of a lot of tasks, one day that person had a mental health breakdown and left and we quickly discovered that no one knew how to turn on the stove. We decided to become geese and rotate jobs, guess what we became a much better team the final two weeks of the trip. So go with expertise on your team but if it is an on-going team, building in cross training will make you better, sometimes the clean-up hitter should hit in the leadoff spot (a baseball metaphor)

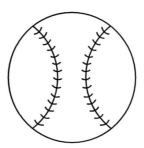

To conclude the thought about the roles, people need to know their roles. Having clarity on roles really helps attend to the human needs on a team, while being flexible builds strength. Assess roles using 5WH: Who does What, When, Where, Why and How, that will give you a real clear picture.

A key factor related to the effectiveness of the team is communication style. Let's face it we have a lot of technology today that is used as a communication tool. The question is how effective is all this technology. Yes team members can work on a document from remote locations in real time. The cell phone with all of its applications means you can send an e-mail to team members 24/7 so that the work day confinement no longer really applies. The trouble is that there seems to be a fatigue factor; everyone is on all the time. I am an old guy and I have four e-mails, facebook, text messages, five different phone numbers where people can leave me a voice mail (actually mostly just robo calls these days as people don't call in the way they used to). The point is there is a ton of communication coming at people and they just cannot catch it all.

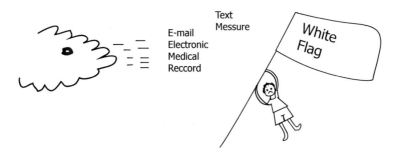

Use this cartoon to motivate you to communicate smartly. One way is to discuss with your team how communication will be handled and what the expectation is regarding communication. I have done this. This is how it goes: I will say, "can we agree, we all will read all the e-mails from team members" "people usually go "of course", then they don't and we have to revisit it. All teams are composed of individuals and every individual has strengths and challenges. Use positive communication to bring forward their strengths for the good of the team. Respectful communication will get you where the team needs to go. Affirmation of others is a free motivator.

Let us talk about conflict on teams for a moment. My direct advice (even though social workers are not supposed to give advice) is to expect some conflict. Actually I think some conflict is good. If everyone is agreeing all the time, more likely than not, people are not being fully invested or honest about what is going on. When you model and communicate that discussion and disagreement are healthy, this allows for more ideas to come forward. Adopting a practice of gaining consensus will help you get there. Many people incorrectly define consensus, it is not everyone agreeing, it is everyone can live with a decision. When you create a team culture where it is ok to disagree and that you work to gain a stance that "I can live with", you now have a team that can achieve, because it will not get bogged down into sidetracks, wordsmithing and hopefully mitigate personality clashes. So here you are following the process of the team. Attack the challenge, just believe the challenge is not a person.

Luft, J. & Ingham, H. (1961). The Johari Window. *Human Relations Training News.* 5, 1, 6-7.

Leadership in teams

When I was a young adult I had a summer job teaching outdoor living skills at a mountaineering camp for boys in the Adirondack Mountains of New York State. The ADKs as they are known are great for hiking with 46 mountains originally known to be over 4,000 feet tall (modern technology have downgraded a few under that mark). One really important lesson I learned was that when attempting to summit a mountain with a team of hikers, it really did not matter what the best hiker could do. It was dangerous and unproductive to the group to have a couple people race up the mountain while the rest lagged behind, we looked like a broken chain.

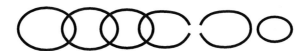

To summit together as a team, the solution was easy; put the slowest walker first. In the beginning this will frustrate the super-fast person but with encouragement and "team affirmations" what happened was a better result for all. What is interesting is that the person that is dragging up the rear, performs much better when put in the lead. That allows me as the leader to take the rear position to make sure that we do not lose anyone or drop any gear along the way. If the group comes to a fork in the road, we can quickly huddle to decide on a course. In the end we summit together and share in our accomplishment together. To be honest, it is more fun to celebrate together, to be an unbroken chain.

A closer examination of the climbing lesson holds some truths for each of us as we lead teams. First is that when we as a leader communicate what we expect from others in a clear and honest fashion, everyone is happier. So many teams struggle because the charge to the team is unclear, or their roles and responsibilities are unclear. Clarity of function and direction will make or break the work and this is a leadership function. As an aside some of the Adirondack high peaks have trails with markers and some do not, leading up an unmarked mountain is a test of leadership. Related to the first point is the importance of delegation of duties. When you delegate, especially if everyone gets a task, then everyone stays involved. In my MSW graduate school work I took a groups class, we were assigned to groups. We got into groups and one woman said "look, I mean no offense, but I have a 4.0 and I am not having you people or this assignment mess it up, so I will do all the work", so we did, I did nothing for that assignment, learned nothing and think of the "A" I got as the perfect example of what is wrong with so many things in our society where we just use the bottom line to determine the effectiveness. Well that is not entirely true, the woman said she had read research that professors give higher grades to papers printed in brown ink, our group paper went in with brown ink, never tried it myself but that factoid always has stayed with me as more evidence of what I don't want to do. The point is, leadership is about getting everyone involved, not standing up on the podium giving a good speech. Delegation done right is not telling people what to do, but getting the team engaged.

This naturally leads us to the world's most dreaded managerial style, the micromanager (I don't have a citation for that, it is just a truth). Quickly let us discuss the good of micromanaging. It is hard to imagine any operation that does not benefit from consistent quality; I will take consistent quality as the aim of anyone who practices a micromanagement leadership approach. There is a line from an old mob genre movie where the head mobster asks the young mobster "would you rather be loved or feared?" with "feared" being the correct answer. I guess if you are running a dangerous crime syndicate being feared probably has its advantages, short of that, working for someone who controls all the decisions all the time is so disempowering that it leads to poor results. Other than the general morale question, micromanagement squashes creativity and innovation. When people are fully engaged in the work of the team and feel they will be heard, you multiply the brain power. More brain power is helpful in dealing with the complex challenges that social work practitioners face.

So what to do instead of micromanage folks? Well you can motivate by promoting the team and its people. Celebrate progress, note good work. Create pride. Just about everyone likes to belong, find ways to have pride and belonging as a team. This is not rocket science, it is having a birthday club, or having food at meetings, do a holiday lunch, organize the team to do a charity walk/run together, write a team mission statement or slogan.

The advice brought to you in the preceding paragraph is straight from the kind folks at "you catch more flies with honey and vinegar" (too gross to draw that one). Positive energy is contagious. When we demonstrate the positive, creative productive work culture we aspire our team to have, we lead the team to be positive and creative and engaged.

It is probably no surprise but I am a big fan of active team building. I like games and I have had the benefit of spending time learning a bunch of adventure-base or experience-based learning games for team building. Today you can go on the web and find lots of games. If you use these types of games, I just wish to offer a few suggestions. First, all games involve some challenge. That said, I encourage you use the "challenge by choice rule". Only we know our bodies, what we are comfortable with and what we are not. The way the rule works is that anyone can opt out of any activity or part of an activity. Now that does not mean that they just go look at their phone, they need to stay engaged as a coach, idea generator or cheerleader. The importance of this rule cannot be understated; I had a student tear her Achilles tendon running literally ten feet on a carpet- it just blew. With that one rule in place, explain the acidity. Next run it. Your job while running the activity is to monitor for safety and to observe the process. The last piece is most important; you need to process with the team the activity. Here I offer a three step post process: First ask people what happened- have them describe the activity- often they solved something; ask them how they did this. Next ask what it was like, try to bring forward the various roles- who were the leaders? How did the team decide who to listen to? Finally get them to apply the activity to the work of the team. The last step is critical as this is where the learning comes from.

In times where an active exercise is not possible or advisable, you can do process activities where you gather the team and ask a series of questions to generate a conversation about the team. Questions such as:

1) What is the best thing each of you can say about our team?

2) What accomplishment of our team are you proudest about?

3) Tell a story where someone of the team had your back

4) Tell a story of how this team got through a difficult moment

Basically the idea is to ask the team open-ended questions to get them processing their work and by the process of hearing each other talk it out, you help to build a positive team culture.

May I close this chapter by directing you to a cool book and a growing body of team leadership. By the latter I am referencing the "servant/authentic leader" literature. In many ways similar to the questions above but with a more self-less undertone if you will. The book will be great for all you Winnie-the-poo fans:

Greenleaf, R. & Spears, L. (2002). *Servant Leadership: A Journey into the Nature of Legitimate Power and Greatness*. Paulist Press: Mahwah, NJ.

Heider, J. (1985) *The Tao of Leadership*. Humanics: Atlanta.

Success on the interprofessional team

If there is anything new in team work these days, it is the focus on the interprofessional team. So many social workers work in settings where there are multiple professionals organized on teams and charged with working together. The advantages of the numerous disciplines working together to the good the person in need of services is obvious. Coordinated care just is better. Plus each profession does have expertise that is different and can be useful in addressing complex challenges. The rub is, that not everyone plays nice in the sandbox, the professional challenge is maximize the opportunity of the various professions.

As a profession, social work brings the art of collaboration to the sandbox. We actually may have more training on how to get along with others than any other profession. As such social workers need to work to make their teams function more collaboratively. Interprofessional teams are especially common in health and behavioral health settings. Social workers can facilitate better services by helping their interprofessinal team stay focused on improving the people we service experience as well as potentially reducing overall cost of care by having for effective and efficient service delivery.

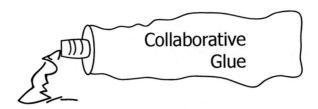

The question is how to avoid turf and ego battles? Here is where your skills are required. You can help build a collaborative environment. There is need for all team members to understand the other professions they work with. You can facilitate a conversation where each profession introduces itself and what they see as their contributions to the work of the team. Clarity creates room in the sandbox. With knowledge what each brings the team is ready to develop shared goals, responsibilities and accountability. The goal is for each profession to feel valued even though they may not make equal contributions. This is that non-summativity thing again; the whole is greater than the simple sum of the parts. The future involves interprofessional teams, be the collaborative glue that binds them together.

Understanding the organization that employs you

For those of you reading this book while in school, it may seem like the education process is going on forever and you cannot wait to graduate. I understand that sentiment, I salute your upcoming achievement but at the same time, I encourage you to see it as just a line, your education is never done. One place where you will need to continue to learn is at the organization that hires you. Understanding how your organization works is a critical practice skill. I am willing to bet that you have all the skills you need to make an assessment of the organization you work for and to adapt your work behavior so you can have a long and successful career there. The key here is to actually do an assessment of your agency. Here is my adaptation of the eco-map concept as an assessment tool. As much as I am sure you have seen my now, I am not maniacal about citation but I totally think that ideas should be credited, to not do so is unethical. Here is the thing, I have been teaching this adaptation of the eco-map drawing to organizations so long, I no longer know where the idea came from. I have searched the internet and do not find it. So I am not claiming it as any great scholarship, I just put some concepts that are important to think about into circles:

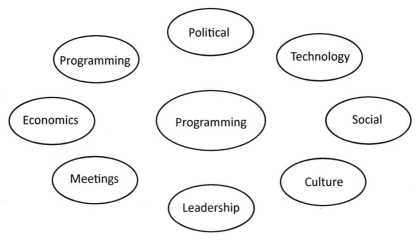

Ok, in a classical eco-map there would be lines between all the circles, if that helps you, by all means go at it, the more you invest in making a map of the organization you work for the more you will get from your efforts. In truth boundaries are a really important topic and there is a lot of fuzziness in the boundaries at work. No doubt there are fuzzy boundaries with regard to the responsibilities of your job. There are most likely a lot of boundary questions about how your agency functions. Departments may overlap in functions or staff. There is a tension, a dynamic in all boundaries, be aware of that tension, watch how the tension shifts, so you can effectively manage boundary issues. From the top then, let us quickly walk through the circles, with the real hope that you will perform a similar analysis in a place where you work or intern.

Political: There are two political realities really, one outside and one inside the agency. You need to attend to both. The external political relates to the reality that surrounds the agency. What do external funders want? How has the political climate about the people your agency serves changed? Here in America we have been in a 1834 Poor law mindset for some time. The effect of an 1834 Poor Law mindset is that services to poor people should not be too easy to obtain, lest the poor become too dependent on the system. Another example has been the shift to having people recover from hospitalization at home, so shorter hospital stays are the norm today, this political reality has an effect on how the organization runs. Internal political realities relate to the strength of programs or people to dominate a conversation. As such it is important to know who or what the dominate political players are and adjust yourself accordingly.

Programming: In today's practice world there is more pressure than ever to use evidence-based models of care. What are the models of care your agency is hanging their hat on? To what degree do they demand fidelity to that model? How is the model trained and supported? Do different parts of the organization have different models or different levels of fidelity? Does the model or models reflect the philosophy of the organizations mission?

Economics: Maybe this seems above your pay grade, but you should know how the agency gets money. What are the sources of money? How stable are those sources? How much of the organizations operating budget comes from grants? Are you on a line that is supported by a grant, or is the funding for your position more secure? You may be interested in the budget, that is fine, this is different, we all should know how the service is funded, local dollars, state money, federal dollars, grants, endowments, gifts.

Meetings: All agencies have meetings. Many social workers spend a good chunk of any given work week in meetings. As such you need to understand how meetings run where you work. Do you have to be on time? Whose meeting would it be very bad to be late for? Do they end on time? Can you talk in meetings

I used to go to a management meeting where the CEO would ask questions, but expect no one to answer- it was good to know that I was not supposed to talk in that meeting. What is the purpose of the meeting? Do you have to do the tasks assigned to you in meetings, because often times, tasks are assigned?

Leadership: There is a lot to say about organizational leadership but let us do a quick and dirty assessment. What would you say is the style of leadership? Is the open door really open? What does the leader expect of you personally and how can you demonstrate that to them? What would make the leader absolutely love your performance? What would make them terminate you- good stuff to know.

Culture: Similar to the political bubble, there is a big C- culture and a little c-culture. The big C relates to the diversity of the work force and how diversity plays out in the work force. What is the diversity make-up of the agency? Are there "glass ceilings" with regard to hiring and promotion? I worked for an organization where there was general acceptance including promotion of lesbian women but real barriers for gay men. How much does the art, the magazines in the waiting room, the board of directors reflect the population that is served by the organization? The work place is one area in America where people representing diverse backgrounds do interact, how does that play out. The little c-culture is more about the nuances of the agency as a place to work. How do you get a private office, or a window or a parking spot? How friendly is the environment?

Social: Closely related to little c-culture is the social environment of the agency. Who mixers with who/ who eats together? Where do people eat? Do people go out after work? Are there organized social event and activities? My own experience with activities has usually worked out poorly, one co-ed softball team put four of my best workers on disability and the annual holiday party held at some local watering hole produced even more disastrous results. I have heard Ophra Winfrey tell her audience that the holiday social is the worst place to ever get drunk- wisdom in my mind.

Technology: So I will admit that I am so old that I completed my MSW using a thing called a type writer with a trusty little bottle of liquid paper by my side to correct my numerous spelling errors, oh how the times have changed. Technology is changing the field for the better in many ways but adding frustrations and the potential for ethical lapses. My advice is to always be ready to learn new technology; there will always be new software programs and innovations. Perhaps you can help your agency use these tools smartly. You can certainly help your agency be mindful on how to protect confidentiality in electronic spaces.

Sacred cows and open communication in agencies

With your assessment complete, I wanted to talk about two more things that could have their own circles two but perhaps need a stand-alone so they are not overlooked: sacred cows and communication within your workplace. We will take the sacred cows thing first. All agencies have these untouchable people and projects. In no way do I mean this in any kind of derogatory way, but there are people and projects that you should just not mess with. Soon I will introduce you to a nun, she was honestly sacred, but due to the length of her service and the pride she had in her work, it was better not to mess with her. Actually this was easy to do, because she was an easy person for pretty much any human being to respect. But there are other folks sprinkled about in every organization, who you should be mindful of and have a strategy so you have a failsafe relationship with them. Some of these people are truly powerful; others could just make your life miserable. Let's take the administrative assistant to the president/CEO of your agency, not a position with a ton of real power, but in fact they do have a ton of real power. In other agencies, there is perhaps an "old timer" who is a little nutty, but has some function that they have done forever. Maybe there is a better way to do that function, but let them be. In addition to people there are always projects that are sacred. It is hard to imagine a CEO that does not have a sacred one. Even if it looks like a dumb idea of fiscal ruin, try to get behind these projects. The point here is that the universal nature of sacred cows in agencies makes them a practice issue to successfully navigate. Gotta draw this one ☺

Cow
Throne

Communication in an agency is as important a practice skill as pretty much any other. Successful communication leads to good practice and happy employees. A lack of successful, open communication in an organization can have major consequences. Confusion, employees feeling isolated, concerns about fair treatment or legal issues from harassment or bias are seen when communication is not successful. Poor communication can break down into outright nastiness in the workplace where infighting and retaliation behaviors emerge. All of the sudden you are working in the worst reality TV show ever.

The most compelling case I can make for the importance of making open and clear communication an organizational priority is that honesty and transparency are the bedrock of an ethical culture. The sad truth is that I have seen too many unethical things go down in organizations and it just saps the strength and morale of the workforce. Gossip begins to rule and the work suffers. People stop taking responsibility and in its blame the blame game emerges. Below is a drawing of the blame game in full swing.

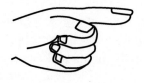

In order to understand how an environment of open communications can motivate agency staff to promote an ethical office culture we need to look a some of the underlying attitudes implicit in ethical conduct. We need more tha compliance which is a form of obedience to the organizations (or the profession code of conduct. That will only lead to surface level ethical conduct. Let me giv you an example: How fast do you drive on a highway where there is a sign that says the speed LIMIT is 55 miles per hour?

```
+-------------------+
|                   |
|   Speed           |
|                   |
|   Limit           |
|                   |
|                   |
|   55              |
|                   |
+-------------------+
```

If we are being honest, most of us drive over the limit (me too). We tell ourselves things to justify this behavior: "Everyone else is going this fast", "I am late", "They don't ticket you until you are going X", "this car is built for speed" and on and on. It is not that we don't know the rule, it is just that it seems to not fully apply. Take the same drivers and have them drive past a kindergarten school that has just let the children out and there are little munchkins running willy nilly all over, chasing balls and butterflies and you may not get to the 20 MPH that the flashing light by the school tells you is the limit. You see the potential consequence of your action and you adjust. This is an example of how a clear understanding of the impact of our actions can modify our behavior and attitude. This is what is needed in organizational communication to ensure ethical practice.

The question is how to promote this concept in an agency? Here leadership has a real challenge to take things on in an ethical way in an expedient manner. I maintain, bad things will happen, you cannot stop all of them, and sometimes we hire people whose behavior is not good for the people we serve or who do not yet have the ability to work well with others. When we show leadership by being clear about the ethical conduct and the ramifications of ethical conduct that are required in the organization, we get people to drive the limit because they see the consequence of their own action. When every staff understands that they have a responsibility to be an early warning system and every supervisor will stop what they are doing and listen to a concern that is being raised, then you can start going in this direction. Every organization should have some type of "red flag" policy that outlines conduct and how to report conduct concerns safely. While it may seem that I have gone on a tangent regarding communication, I maintain, if you want good organizational communication, setting safe and communication practices and procedure around ethical lapses is the necessary first building block.

The power of "Yes"

YES

This is a chapter about one word that when properly applied will make your life as a social work practitioner so much better. We hear so much about burnout in the field, this one word can help with that. We hear so much about the unending demands, the pressure, the pace, well this one word can help with that too.

Make no mistake; this is a chapter about personal philosophy. I did not learn this in graduate school. I learned this from years of working. Watching what worked for me and others and watching what did not work for others. What ended up making this all come so clear to me is that I worked in a child welfare agency that had been started by an order of nuns, there was one sister left when I worked there. She had been a nun for 64 years, an amazing lady but she was imposing. She and I did enjoy a good respectful relationship and I asked her "what was the secret of her success of such a long work history in a highly stressful environment?" In addition to her faith, she said she makes it a practice to use the word "yes" when asked to do things. This became our collective practice, in fact my director when he was promoted had this painted on his wall: "Yes, and how can we make it happen?"

So let us unpack this concept some so as to not suggest simply solutions to complex challenges. By and large the people that are drawn to this field are doers, natural helpers, people with a desire to make this place a better place, to improve lives. Our collective orientation to the field and to the work defines us as professionals. Along the way however, negativity has a way of worming its way in and disrupting us and our ability to complete our personal mission. This does not happen overnight, it is much more insidious than that. You see excellent professionals starting to develop alligator arms, where they no longer fully grab the work. Alligators are powerful animals that have thrived for millennials, but are challenged by having short arms so they cannot grab onto much. Here is my drawing of a short-armed alligator:

What you see is folks "just getting through". They watch the clock they tell themselves things will be better next month, or after so and so leaves, or if they get rid of this case, or after they have a vacation. Not that there is not some truth to these ideas, but in fact the challenge is deeper. The challenge relates to how the orientation to the work has been shifted by the powerful forces that we encounter; trauma, bureaucracy, mixed success, increasing paperwork including computer applications that leave us staring at a screen for chunks of the day. For me, the way to continued success has been to say "yes". As paradoxical as it sounds, I have found that taking on an extra task, especially a quirky- even a "fool's errand", has been professionally invigorating. People ask me to do things all the time; I try to say "yes" whenever possible. As hippy-dippy as it sounds, surrounding myself with positive energy has made it so I do get out of bed every day and look forward to going to work, because I love being a social worker. This is basically a question of fuel. What puts gas in your tank?

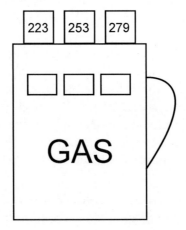

Your social work suit

In the last chapter on the word "yes" I introduced you to an older nun. While she was not a direct social work practice mentor, she did mentor me with regard to the power of yes. Then I noticed something else. The main campus of the child welfare organization we worked for had once been a farm. All the farm buildings were gone and replaced by the buildings for the child welfare organizations except for the barn. The barn had been converted into space to house the buildings and grounds crew (which makes sense), and to house the food services for the children. The food services were run by the nun in question. In addition to her duties running the food services, the nun had planted roses around the edge of the barn between the building and the parking lot that now surrounded the barn. Mostly red rose plants but some yellow and pink varieties as well. The barn sits in the Northeastern United States in a town that averages 100 inches a snow a year. I noticed that sister's roses bloomed from summer into January. They are just amazingly productive roses. I never knew if they were so productive because she knew a lot about growing roses or she had a connection to a higher source ☺.

To get to work each day I had to drive past the barn and the roses to park my car. To leave work each day I had to do the same. I adopted a mental routine that when I saw the roses in the morning, I was "on" as a social worker. Below is one of sister's roses. When I left for the day I would consciously look at the roses and tell myself I was "off" as a social worker, and only go back on if I was called at home (as on-call was a duty) or when I saw the roses next. In this way I had a planned way of putting my "social work suit" on and taking it off. Both are important.

Here is the argument for turning yourself on. Our work is stressful. Increasingly the scientific exploration of stress is showing that we as people carry the stress with us and, in general, stress is not good for our physical and mental selves. One way to buffer the effects of stress is to be ready for it. Having a way of consciously turning yourself on becomes protective. Think about it as an engagement activity. When you start with someone, even when you have been working together for a long time, you do some kind of engagement check in (as we discussed earlier, this is essential for good practice). You should expect the same for yourself. There are many ways to do this. The visual imagery I use is just one way, and this is just a suggestion, but my belief is that you will be more effective, more on point, if you ready yourself, if you actively find a way to put your suit on.

Here is the argument for turning yourself off. This is not a suggestion, it is a command, you gotta turn it off. Your personal life demands that you turn it off. Trust me on this, your love interest and your family do not want you to diagnosis them. Sometimes however, the things that happen during the day, you have to process. First I hope you have the opportunity for supervision to do so. A second idea is to use the time you are transporting yourself from the work space to the living space to review the day and try to make sense of it. The point is that your neurons need to go off alert status. I am a mandated reporter that means from time to time, I am in the grocery store or some public space where I see a person I do not know disciplining a child in a way that would require me to make a report. This is always hard, I try to put the suit on real quick and figure out what to do. This is what I know, in a public place, when people are amped up, the last thing they want is a stranger interfering in their business. I use this knowledge to make a quick assessment of how vital it is for me to say something, and then try a soft approach such as "my kids were famous for pulling spaghetti sauce jars off the shelf to disastrous effect" to see if I can interrupt the process. Twice, I have felt compelled to step into a domestic violence situation that erupted. Both times it worked but people with me told me I was going to get killed doing that. I tell you these stories so you know that I know that it is not always so neat and tidy to turn it off. I get that, but on a day to day basis, you have to find a way to turn it off. To leave work at work, and if you have to turn it back on, turn it off again as soon as you can.

One final, perhaps unrelated thought, but it pertains to our "suit". I find it helpful to dress the same way when I go to work. The consistency helps others view me as consistent and helps me be in the mode to do the work. In America we are progressing towards a business casual in many jobs. This has advantages and disadvantages. What to wear to work is a good subject to explore As we have progressed as a society there is a lot more latitude in what to wear, 40 years ago it was suit and tie for the gents, dress and hose for the ladies. That fixed idea of what to wear has moved. First I think you need to think about whom are you dressing for? I hope that is the people you work with. I do think that we are professionals and we should come across that way. At the same time if we are too flashy that can be off-putting. That said culture plays a role. There is that "dress for success motto". This reflects on you being you. The point here is what do you do? What is the norm in your work place? How are you going to dress?

So take a moment here and write it down. I find that setting an intention is a good way to direct our practice. So I am purposefully leaving some room right here on the page for you to write down how you are going to dress- in general for work. It is ok to write in this book, write in pencil if you are borrowing it, but write down you intention.

I plan on usually dressing in this way_____

___

It makes sense to me that we look respectful at all times. That conveys that the people we work with are worthy of us looking respectful. My colleague Annmarie has the rule of the "three B's- no bellies, butts or boobs". So do not dress like you would if you were going to the club or the beach. If you are more well to do, be mindful of how much expensive jewelry you wear. Some of us do not like the business causal, please, by all means, look good. Many men really enjoy the style of tie- that is excellent, others find them uncomfortable ketchup, mustard and salad dressing attractors (that's me below with my hand up). Sure if I am going to court, I wear a tie, but everyday no. I don't even like wearing ties when I get dressed up for a wedding or some formal occasion. I have tons of ties; I try to pawn them off on my brother or my nephews. That said a lot of men like wearing ties. Either way look respectable and consistent in your social work suit, and turn it on and definitely off at the end of the workday.

Two Trees

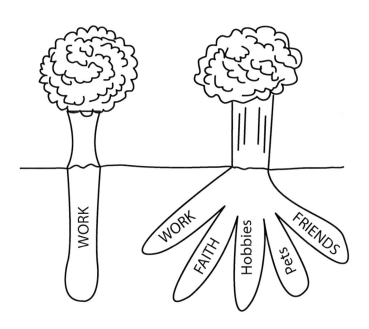

There once was a forest and in that forest there were these two trees that had come up together, gone to school together, entered the tree profession together and generally got along well. They felt they had made the right choice in being trees and in fact they were similar in many ways. They did have one main difference between them. One tree just had one main root. The root was named "social work". The other tree had several roots. It too had a root named "social work" but it also had a root named "friends", one named "family", one named "running" another named "book group", another named "missy the cat", maybe a newer root called "yoga". You get the picture. Anyway, things in the forest were quite fine for a while but then as increasingly tends to happen, an invasive species entered the forest. The species was the feared root-eating beetle, pictured below:

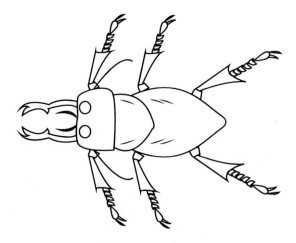

So which tree is more vulnerable to the invasive species? The single rooted tree of course! This chapter is meant as a cautionary tale. You are in the right place in your life. You are doing the right work. In order to do this work along time, I tell my students that my goal is to be a social worker 40 years (I am getting close) and my goal for them is the same 40 years. To do that, to do this work for that long, to have a lifelong career, you have to have balance in your life. All the things that are you, that describe you, which you also have passion for, are critical to your success and longevity as a social worker. I will end with a little plug for yoga. The trees, while they can bend, perhaps cannot do cat and cow, but you can. Here I am doing Cat and them Cow. There is a growing science to back what the East has known for centuries. Our body is a better temple when we stretch it and when we are mindful of our breath. Just think of time on a mat as not a competition of who can look best in their yoga pants or who can do what positon best but rather as time you give yourself because you are so worth it.

At the end of the day, whether you do yoga or not, have a lot of roots. The non-social work roots will help your social work root stay healthy and strong and able to fight off the root eating beetles of the world.

On being organized

Having a long and successful career as a social worker involves you staying sane. Part of maintaining your sanity is being an organized social worker. I am talking about having an organized way in which you come to work. See if you can arrive around the same time. Some jobs make this harder to do than others- they require more flexibility, so of course you should follow the norm in that situation but if you in a more traditional setting try to arrive at the same time. For me that was a little early so I could get myself ready. Many of the social workers I talk to or have supervised would say that it is not the work with the people that is so hard it is all the other stuff. Largely we are talking about what we used to call paperwork but now really are better called computer work for most social workers. Along with the computer work is answering phone messages and e-mails, all of which can quickly pile up. Below is your basic social worker at their desk, buried, but with a plan.

The key word here is to have a plan, have a way of getting this stuff done. In some ways, this is similar to wearing the same kind of outfit to work. The truth is the more organized you are at work, the more you will feel competent and the more others will see you as competent. Some of this may be unearned, but if you have a system so you get your work done, you can keep doubt about your ability at bay and others will see you as the person you really knows what they are doing. On the flip side, one of the most frequent reasons I have seen professional social workers terminated from employment is consistent timeliness in reporting issues. Increasingly today, funders are demanding documentation within 24 hours of service provision. With the introduction of Electronic records in many settings, funders can see compliance and failure to comply with regulation, and this makes you vulnerable. One helpful way to think about this is to think of your documentation time as time where you can reflect on the case. Often the session goes by so quickly you need some time to put it all together, by consciously reflecting on the work while documenting, you build in some self-directed practice skills. Other methods that are frequently employed are to develop written checklists of tasks for more complicated practices, for instance all the forms involved in an intake. Other people like to color code with sharpies various duties. Others like to keep a list that they check off. Anyway you do it that works for you is good, being haphazard is bad because it leaves you vulnerable to missing things. I tell you all this and I must confess, I am slow to pick up computer-based technology. I need to do things several times before I get the hang of it and usually am months behind learning the computer-based shortcuts that folks that get technology well, know on day one. This is all the more reason I need a system, without a system, I would get buried.

You have to post

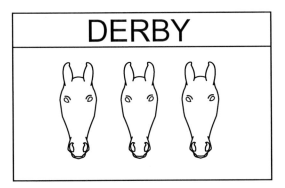

DERBY

This is a drawing of a group of horses in the post ready to run a race- think Kentucky Derby. This will be a brief chapter extolling the virtue of showing up to work, rolling up your sleeves and getting it done, again and again. It is no accident that the word "work" is in our professional title. Yes a good number of us spend much of the day sitting in a chair but what we do is heavy lifting. The emotional weight of our work is physically exhausting, which is why we need to practice self-care. That said, we need to have strong work ethics. So many of the people we work with are challenged with issues of loss. When we are inconsistent, it just reinforces the lack of permanence of people in the world, that leads to feelings of alones and lack of safety. The people we have the honor of working with need us to post, to be there for them. They need us to be PROFESSIONALS. To do that we have to show up and be ready to work and do what is required to do. If there is one critique of our profession that seems to be accurate it is that we move around too much, that we change jobs every couple of years, that we can't be satisfied or we burn out on the work too quickly. Use your self-care to fight the urge to believe that the grass is greener or the wine is sweeter. There is real satisfaction in long-term consistent service. Not to throw a stone, but those of you born post 1988 have been criticized as not having the work ethic of the older generations. That may or may not be true, your generation has had to face things and wake up each day to more choices than any prior generation. Still, beat the stereotype back by posting and being a model social worker.

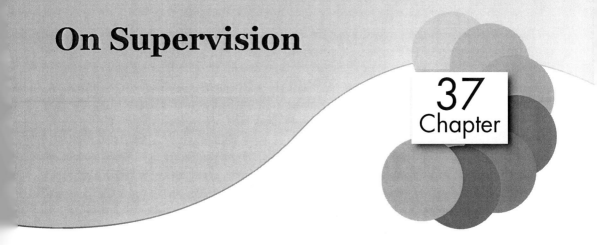

On Supervision

Chapter Thirty Seven

On Supervision

In the olden days when you wanted to build a house, you went out into the field and found four large flat rocks that would be the cornerstones of your home,

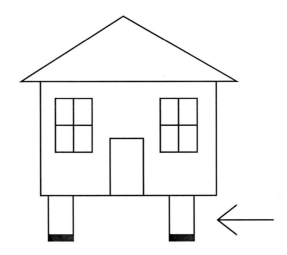

Supervision is the cornerstone of our profession. Yes it is not billable. Most likely it is not an evidenced-based practice either; it is just the most important hour of your week. Here is hoping that you get supervision and it is an hour. Here is hoping your supervisor and your agency still values supervision. I have had some bad supervisors, but I also have had some excellent ones- in graduate school, Denise R., for nine years in NYC Sue G., Dr. F and Dr. B, then later after I moved from New York, a great boss in Bill and wisdom of a psychologist Dr. Gene. I mention names because I would not be here now writing this book, teaching social work or being a good (if I can be so modest) clinical social worker. I was once green as they come, bumbling, full of energy but rough, rough, rough. It was supervision that developed me. That is what supervision is intended to be: development work. It should be challenging, it should make you think. It is a process. It is a process that requires everyone to do their part. Supervision requires a supervisor to spend time engaging their worker so they get to know them. The supervisor needs to value the time, so that interruptions are limited. Mostly what is need is the creation of safe space, so the worker can be vulnerable. The work has a way of getting to us, having safe space to process it and make sense and to plan is essential to good practice. For me that translated into wanting to give back to those I had the good fortune of supervising, what had been given to me. Sue G. had required me to bring an agenda to supervision, she was always ready, and she wanted to hear about my cases and my thoughts on what was happening. Together we would develop a map of intervention to maintain motivation and progress. That was the blueprint I used. Perhaps one of the greatest compliments I ever got was one a performance evaluation from my boss Bill who wrote "the world could be ending from an atomic bomb attack and Jed will still stick to his supervision schedule". I love being a social worker and although I do have some genetic loading (my mom was the first HIV/AIDS social worker in our city), it is clear as a bell to me that I was made into a social worker. It was my clients as my first teachers and my supervisors as my second teachers and schooling with the bronze medal.

So the question is "what is your responsibility as supervisee?" Well glad you asked. The answer is simple; the more you put into supervision the more you will get out of it. You are responsible for a good amount of the safety in the room. Come to supervision honestly. Own the work, own the mistakes, make yourself vulnerable. We ask the people we work with to be vulnerable with us, it is only fair that we be able to do the same in supervision. If you make yourself vulnerable and your supervisor cannot treat that vulnerability like the gift that it is, shame on them. I do get fired up about this, but if we do not like some of the ways our profession is becoming homogenized, then one thing we can do is stand loud and proud about the things that make us great. Supervision is a practice that makes us great. I was raised to come to supervision with an agenda of what I wanted to talk about. The idea being is that if I did some reflective work before I walked in the door, I was in a better place to use the precious time. As we have discussed, our own organization is key to our success. This is certainly true with regard to supervision, coming to supervision in a thoughtful and organized manner, means you will get more out of supervision. The truth about our work is that there is always so much happening, on so many levels: engagement, assessment, diversity, content, process, safety, trust, history and so forth, that no one person, no matter how good they are, can catch all of it. Supervision is intended to be a reflective space to make sense out of all that is going on with the work. It also can be a place where I hope you can process what it is like being an employee where you are working, being a team member with the teams you are on, there is so much to tall about. Ultimately it is my wish that supervision becomes a place where you can plot out the arc of your professional career. The point here is to encourage you to take the reins and do just that.

One final thing I want to pass along as I tell all my graduating students this final thought about supervision. When you are starting out, if you have multiple options for jobs, I would take the job with the best supervisor over best pay or the work I like most, in the long run, the supervision will pay like gold for you as it has for me.

The Dash

Here Lies
Jed Metzger

1961 - ?

Well we have come to the end of this book, I hope you have found it useful, actually I hope you will continue to find it useful. Our work is hard, it is challenging and that is a good thing. The point of this final drawing is to highlight that fact. See we are all born and we all will pass on, in between is what matters. That is the dash- the time between birth and whatever comes after we leave this earth, and that matters. It does matter that you have chosen this field. It does matter that you have chosen to do work in service of others. What we do is important. It is challenging but fulfilling because it is honest work. You and the work you do have good purpose. You will leave the world a better place. This is not hyperbole, most likely the goodness of your work will be slow, like grass growing, but it is important none-the-less. My wish for you is to enjoy whatever field of practice you find yourself engaged in. Know that is the good work. Go forth and do it.